*How to
Buy and Sell
Real Estate
for Financial
Security*

How to
Buy and Sell
Real Estate
for Financial
Security

ROBERT IRWIN

McGRAW-HILL BOOK COMPANY

New York   St. Louis   San Francisco   Auckland   Düsseldorf
Johannesburg   Kuala Lumpur   London   Mexico   Montreal
New Delhi   Panama   Paris   São Paulo   Singapore
Sydney   Tokyo   Toronto

Library of Congress Cataloging in Publication Data

Irwin, Robert, 1941-
  How to buy and sell real estate for financial security.

  Includes index.
  1. Real estate investment.   2. Real estate investment—United States. I. Title.
HD1375.I77   332.6'324   75-9814
ISBN 0-07-032063-2

    67890 BPBP 784321098

*The editors for this book were W. Hodson Mogan and Carolyn Nagy,
the designer was Naomi Auerbach, and the production supervisor
was Teresa F. Leaden. It was set in Electra
by University Graphics, Inc.*

It was printed and bound by The Book Press.

For Reet and the Boys

Contents

4. Don't Be Overwhelmed by Real Estate Forms   71

5. How to Successfully Borrow Money on Real Estate   85

6. How to Invest in Groups   127

7. The "Repo" Market   142

8. Real Estate Tax Shelters and Tax Problems   153

9. Eleven Great Investment Opportunities   171

Preface

If you are out of work and have no money in the bank and few assets, there is very little this book can do for you (although it can show you how you may qualify to buy a house: see Chapter 5). If, however, you work for a living or have a little money in the bank that you are willing to invest, it can show you how to make large profits in real estate.

If you are like most people, you are feeling the effects of inflation and recession. That means that your paycheck shrinks a little each week even though the figures on it remain the same. It also means that it seems to cost you an arm and a leg when you want to borrow money to buy a car or a TV. It means that when you put your money in the bank at the highest interest rate per year (the highest rate available at this writing is 7½ percent), you are still losing to inflation. (You could lose much more if you did not bank at those high rates.) It means that *unemployment* can suddenly threaten you in a completely unexpected manner. It means shortages of gas or wheat can suddenly skyrocket prices and throw auto workers or food processors out of work. It means shortages of what were once considered easily purchased necessities such as gas, bread, and meat. It means no one who works for wages is secure. It means that the "good life" we as Americans have come to take for granted is ending and now it is time to make ourselves battle-ready to weather any impending economic attack on us, personally.

For some this takes the form of inviting the boss to dinner twice a year, instead of just once, or of buying more life insurance. For others, however, this can be a time of great opportunity. They will not simply try to pad what they already have, but use the times to acquire much, much more.

Of late I have heard the excuse "But times are tough." The answer to such a statement is that for those without the determination to make things better, the times will always be tough.

Often the same person asks, "I don't know how—who do I turn to?" Who can really see the way out of this economic quagmire? Here the answer has to be that we must turn to ourselves. No one can teach you how to be financially secure. Guidelines can be given, of course, as they are later in Chapter 1, but ultimately you must solve your own economic problems. The important thing is to understand that in today's world you are losing ground by just standing still.

Of course, you don't want to do anything rash. In unprecedented times such as these it is the prudent person who acts *cautiously* Caution, playing it on the safe side, is always good advice when the way ahead is unclear Many people, however, concerned with inflation or worried about their future employment and security, have acted incautiously. They have attempted to find an easy way out in a variety of get-rich-quick fields. Among these are the commodity market (including gold and silver), rare coins and paintings, antiques, rare books, even old vending and slot machines. (For a detailed analysis of the perils of each of these fields see the end of Chapter 9.)

A true investor in any of these fields is one who either can use the commodity involved or has a true appreciation and love for the objects purchased. Anyone else who buys in is just a speculator. More often than not, he "buys high," because he does not know the field, and then waits hoping the price will go up so he can sell even higher. If the price drops, as it has done on occasion within the last five years in every field mentioned, he can be wiped out. The speculator here is really out to make a quick dollar and is braving heavy risks to do it. Unfortunately, stories of those who lost money are seldom told, while tales of those who made fortunes are often repeated. One large commodity brokerage firm in Chicago, for example, conducted an informal and confidential study of all its "speculative" investors over the last ten years. It concluded that fully 85 percent lost all the money they invested—yes, *all* the money. Of course the other 15 percent did very well. Always, in these fields, the expert is in a position to know what to buy and when to buy, and most often he makes his profits from the novices' losses. And someone driven in by inflation or job insecurity is a perfect definition of a novice.

There is one field, however, where that rule does not apply. That is real estate. Here it is possible for the absolute beginner, one who has never bought before, to make his future secure. Here it is possible to make large sums of money in a relatively short period of time, with almost no risk. This book will tell you why and show you how.

The author wishes to thank the following for their invaluable suggestions and aid in preparing this book: Richard Brickman, attorney; Edwin Duncan, attorney; Norman Lane, professor of tax law at the University of Southern California; Leo Wolenik, Realtor; James Bambrick, investment counselor; Gunther Bahrs, artist, and James Miller, publisher of COINage magazine for his kind understanding and support.

DISCLAIMER

The reader should take careful note of this disclaimer. This book should not be construed as providing legal or tax advice. The reader should not rely on any legal or tax material in this book. Since it would be impossible to anticipate all the myriad financial situations that individuals find themselves in, the investor should consult with his own attorney, financial adviser, and/or accountant for answers to questions about any specific investments he may be considering or may be making. The purpose of this book is to bring to the attention of the reader the possibilities for profit that exist in buying and selling real estate today.

Robert Irwin

Introduction:

Is Your Standard of Living Going Down?

John Piersons should not be out of work. Yet he has not been able to find suitable employment for a year and a half. He is thirty-nine years old, has a stable home life with a wife and two growing children, is in perfect health, and even has a college degree in business. John's problem is that he is a stockbroker and was swept out with the "gloom and doom" of the market fall in early 1974. The last job he held was as a salesperson in a shoe store. When I talked with him he had just quit—it paid only $80 a week, and so he was going back to school to get his teaching credentials. Bad move, I suggested. There are thousands of unemployed teachers looking for work. He just shrugged and said, "What else can I do?"

Of course there were many things he could have done, but in his state of mind at the time, depression ruled them all out. He only hoped to make enough money, with his wife working, to get from day to day. Dimly he hoped that a teaching job sometime in the future would solve everything.

If John Piersons' situation were unique it could be dismissed, but unfortunately in the last few years he has become something of a typical case. In 1965 who would have thought that an aerospace engineer would become an unemployable element in the job market? Or that an alliance of the oil-producing nations in the Middle East would force gasoline prices to skyrocket and eventually result in hundreds of thousands of auto workers being unemployed, some permanently? Or that the sale of American wheat to Russia would trigger a shortage of grains and other foods causing prices to soar upward, resulting in thousands in the food-processing industry being laid off (and indirectly threatening the very existence of the small American farmer)? Or that increased costs of lumber and other building materials coupled with "tight money" would produce unemployment in the construction industry? Or that rampant inflation caused in large part by gasoline and food price increases would send the cost of borrowing money to its highest level since the American Civil War, staggering the financing industry and threatening to throw thousands more out of work?

These are the big examples, but there are countless others. We are living in unprecedented times. On one hand we have a great many employed individuals (take a lineman for a utility company, for example, who makes between $12,000 and $14,000 a year) who can afford the payments on a house, a new car, or a color television set, and on the other hand an out-of-work stockbroker who cannot afford to have his family eat meat more than once a week.

But even if John Piersons were employed, he would face some imposing economic problems. In 1974 the rate of inflation was 12.2 percent. In his last job as a stockbroker he was making roughly $23,000 a year. Unless he had received a raise of about 12 percent or $2,760 he would have lost money just keeping the same job in 1975. And if he had received that raise and deposited it all in the bank at the highest interest rates then available, or 7½ percent, on four-year certificates of deposit, he would still be losing about 3½ percent on his money.

If he could have taken the money and bought stocks (which he certainly would not have done, being a broker and knowing what was happening), he would probably have lost anywhere from 10 to 50 percent of his money by the year's end. If he had bought bonds or any type of security, unless he could make over 10 percent (which was possible), he would be standing still. Only if he had invested his money in highly speculative markets such as coins, antiques, rare paintings, or precious metals could he have made a profit, perhaps as high as 50 percent (compared, of course, with a risk factor of as high as 50 percent).

And being an outsider to these fields and having to rely on others' advice, what chance did he really have to be in the 50 percent that made the profit?

John Piersons' problem was that even before he lost his job he was in a recession. Just by standing still, in a few years his standard of living would have deteriorated to below acceptable levels.

And while John Piersons is only one individual, every worker in America who depends solely on his job for his income is in the same boat—a brightly painted showboat with a slow leak in its hull sinking irresistibly in a financial quagmire.

It is to the John Piersonses that this book is dedicated. There is a way, a safe way without any great inconvenience, to make money, a lot of money, in real estate. I know of at least a dozen people who have done it. I am doing it myself today. There is no reason that your doing it will in any way prevent me or anybody else from doing it. But it does require an understanding that we are living in *unprecedented times*, and we have to rethink all our old notions about what is happening to real estate and money in this country.

1

Real Estate —
the Great American Road to Wealth

Real estate is the one field of investment where it is possible for the total beginner to win the first time and every time; where the working man can make his fortune secure. For in real estate it is possible to purchase a substantial piece of property, put up as little as 5 percent of the purchase price in your own money, do so with virtually no risk and be almost certain that when you sell, the money you get back will at the *very least* have kept up with inflation. But it is more likely that you will make a large profit. Just ask anyone who has ever bought a home and he or she will bear out the simple truth of this statement.

Of course, there is nothing new in this. Real estate has always been the most secure investment possible. However, methods of investing in real estate have changed considerably. Let us consider a few success stories of the past. John Jacob Astor was probably America's first real estate entrepreneur. He came to America in 1783 as an immigrant from Germany and at first had to rely on his brother's charity to survive. Yet within a few dozen years he grew to become America's, perhaps the world's, richest man of that age. He did it largely by buying property. He had no secret plan or inside information; he did what was obvious. He bought on the outskirts of Manhattan Island and waited until the city grew up around his property; then he sold.

Of course, in Astor's day, he was virtually the only one doing this, and consequently he succeeded. Today any reasonable person given the opportunity to buy a lot on the edge of New York at Maine farm prices would jump at the chance. Today the investing public is much more sophisticated than in Astor's time.

During the dark days of the great depression of the 1930s (and earlier in the great depression of the 1880s and what was probably America's greatest depression in the 1830s) enterprising individuals once again made fortunes in real estate. And once again there was no "secret way" or "insider's information" to their method. There was, however, a great deal of "guts." They bought up foreclosed property from banks at prices sometimes as low as 25 cents on the dollar. They rented the property ruthlessly to make their loan payments, hung on to it, and then, when the depression ended, sold for eight to ten times the price they had paid. If and when we enter our next depression, the same method will probably work again.

In the 1950s, times changed once again and so did investors' techniques. The fifties brought a period of enormous expansion and boom to America, and real estate was on the leading edge, as witness the two types of people who obtained great wealth from property during this period, Mr. Gamble and Mr. Dominick.

Mr. Dominick (not his real name) came to the United States as an emigrant in 1913. His homeland had been Austria-Hungary (a country that has since ceased to exist), where with his seven brothers and four sisters he managed to survive on the family farm. But World War I was brewing, and to avoid being drafted into the kaiser's army— first, to fight for a cause he did not believe in, and second, to face a high risk of death—he fled to America. Here he was drafted and served a year in France.

Upon returning to the United States, Mr. Dominick drifted to California and the melting pot of San Francisco, where he worked in a butcher shop. Over a period of years he saved a sum of money and then moved down to the prune orchards of the Santa Clara Valley some 50 miles south. Here he did what came naturally. He worked on a farm, picked prunes, and held on to his money.

Eventually he married and used the money he had saved plus a dowry he received to buy a small farm of his own—just 20 acres. And there he sat. During the dark days of the thirties, when a neighbor who had a farm with a mortgage on it was forced into default, Mr. Dominick picked that up, adding another 11 acres to his land. After this, nothing exciting happened to him economically until 1953. In that year a man came to him and said, "I can make you a fortune— more money than you've ever dreamed of—all we have to do is subdivide your land, build houses, and sell them. No one eats prunes anymore," Mr. Dominick was told, "but everyone needs a house, and your land is in such a good location they will be willing to pay plenty."

There was only one catch. The speaker—we shall call him John Gamble—said he was just starting as a builder and did not have the cash to buy; but he did have enough cash to put down, say, $1,000 on each *acre* and give a loan for the balance if Dominick would agree to subordinate that loan to a later construction loan to be given to Gamble by a bank, by means of a *subordination clause* (see the Glossary of Most Commonly Used Real Estate Terms for definitions). He would be paid off in full when the houses to be built were sold.

What Mr. Gamble did not point out was that if for any reason he was unable to sell the houses he had built, the bank that gave that construction loan would foreclose and probably leave Dominick without an additional cent to compensate for the loss of his property.

What made Dominick's ears perk up was the fact that Mr. Gamble was willing to pay him $10,000 an acre. For 31 acres that meant $310,000. His profit and loss sheet would look like this:

Paid for 31 acres	probably less than $2,000
In cash now $31,000	31 acres at $1,000 an acre
In cash when houses sold	$279,000
Profit	$310,000

Mr. Dominick could not wait to sign on the dotted line. More than a quarter-million dollars, and that was in terms of 1950 dollars, which bought considerably more than our dollars buy today.

Mr. Dominick did not consider the risks; he was not even aware of them, and this was probably a good thing because he just might not have sold if he had known them. Mr. Gamble did build on the property—eight houses to every acre—and within two years they were all sold and Mr. Dominick retired in Orange County with his money. He was one type of individual to make a real estate fortune in the fifties.

Another type was Mr. Gamble. The houses he built sold for $17,500, a fair price in those days. However, they did not cost Mr. Gamble $17,500 to build. Here is the expense sheet for his homes:

Land	$1,200 per lot (eight lots per acre at $10,000 an acre)
Improvements	$1,000 sewers, streets, grading, utilities)
Building costs	$12,000 (1,200 square feet at $10 a foot—building was cheap during the early fifties)
Sales	$550 (Mr. Gamble had a blanket contract with a broker and an escrow title insurance company. He paid one rate for each house.)
Total	$14,750
Sales price	$17,500
Profit	$2,750

He was making $2,750 on each home sold. A tidy profit, you might think, until you remembered that there were eight houses per acre and a total of 31 acres, or 248 houses, or a sum of $682,000 profit. Mr. Gamble had done quite well for himself on his investment of $31,000. His case and Mr. Dominick's were not isolated incidents. Many made less and others made more.

Needless to say, conditions today are different. In the 1970s we have had inflation. This has resulted in a shortage of loan money and has caused what is available to be very expensive in terms of interest per year charged. In addition the cost of labor in the building industry has itself tripled, not to mention the increased price of building materials. Today it would be virtually impossible for a Mr. Gamble to build a large tract of similar homes for even twice the price he was then asking.

We also are plagued by a recurring and occasionally severe recession in which select groups of individuals are left unemployed. This has happened in the automotive field, teaching, space, engineering, the stock market, the paper industry, and a dozen other areas. There simply are not as many buyers with large amounts of money to spend as there were a few years ago. Even if Mr. Gamble could build his tract today, it is doubtful that with selective unemployment and high interest rates he could find large numbers of purchasers. And finally, there just are not too many Dominicks (who bought land years ago and just held on to it) left.

Does this mean that there are few opportunities for the average individual to invest in real estate today? Not at all; it simply means that to be successful today requires understanding and adapting to today's market. There is no secret way or insider's information that will make you great profits in real estate today. There is common sense.

Probably the reason I have most often heard for not investing in real estate today is lack of knowledge. Let us make a comparison. If you want to buy stock, you simply go to any stockbroker and in a matter of moments he arranges the transaction. The same holds true for Treasury notes or bonds and also for commodities such as tin, potatoes, or silver. But to buy real estate for investment, even with the aid of a broker, involves seemingly complicated financing, difficult-appearing legal forms, and often belligerent buyers, sellers, agents, etc., who can place emotionally charged blocks in the path of simple transactions.

Because the demand for real estate investment is so great, however, two simple solutions have come into vogue in the last ten years. Unfortunately, both have serious drawbacks. They are the REIT (real estate investment trust) and syndication. (Both will be discussed in detail in Chapter 6.) The REIT is like a corporation (but with specific legal limitations and tax advantages). You buy stock in a simple transaction through a broker, and the REIT invests your money in either real estate or real estate loans. You share in the profits via the dividends. The profits of the REITs in the later sixties tended to be in the 7 to 10 percent range, providing a good return for those days. But with the recessions and inflations of the seventies their profits plunged, causing numerous investors to "bail out."

Syndications, or limited partnerships, were popular in the early 1970s. Here investors would pool their money to buy a bigger piece of real estate than any of them could afford separately. For example, ten investors could pool $10,000 each and get together enough money ($100,000) to make a down payment on a $400,000 building, much more than any single investor with $10,000 could swing. In addition, there are great tax advantages to syndications, and this led to their downfall. Many individuals invested large sums of money with the inducement that they would save on their income tax. Too often, while they did save some on taxes, the project went "belly up" and they lost their original investment. It is not considered good sense to spend $10 and get back $5, yet that is what happened.

Good syndications are still available, but they tend to be few and far between and also to be in small offerings of ten persons or less; and unless you have a friend who asks you in, it is difficult to find them. The other problem with syndications is that while profits can be good—15 to 20 percent a year on the investment—they do not compare with the much larger profits available to those who invest on their own.

But how can an individual who has no experience or knowledge of the real estate field invest on his own? The answer to that question is in this book. It is a layman's guide to real estate. Here *is* everything you should need to know to make large profits in a relatively short time without great risk or great investment. And it works during periods of recession or inflation.

It must be noted, however, that while this book is geared to investing during a recession or inflation, this does not mean that the techniques described will not work during periods of "boom." They will work even better then. The point is, they will also work when times are bad.

The prudent investor today can *use* inflation and the selective unemployment of a recession to his or her advantage. *Without increasing one's risk or investment* it is possible to make a very large profit in a relatively short time. It does not take above-average luck or superintelligence or an ear to someone "in the know." It does take common sense and an understanding of how the real estate field operates. In Chapter 2 we discuss how an actual couple aware of these opportunities used them to turn $1,500 into $230,000 in a relatively short time in real estate. But first, let us examine the three guidelines that this couple, Gail and Howard VanTill, unknowingly followed. Although they never wrote them down, they are noted here for the convenience of the reader so that he or she can refer back to them and see how Gail and Howard used them in their progress toward wealth.

1. *Use inflation as a psychological tool.*

There is no absolute value to a piece of property. Its value is what someone will pay for it. Today people have learned to live with high inflation and have been conditioned to think of the price of every-thing as going up dramatically. This means that buyers, particularly in higher-priced areas, no longer check sales of two or three years earlier to see if the price they are paying is reasonable. They *assume* that regardless of what a house sold for a few years ago, it will sell for much more today. Hence it is possible to purchase a house that is priced low because of certain devaluing conditions, correct the deval-uing conditions, and sell for as much as twice what you paid.

2. Take advantage of the unusual financing available today.

Today's conditions are relatively new. Financial institutions, including the government through its FHA (Federal Housing Administration) and GI programs, have not really adjusted. Consequently, the financing available today was designed to meet conditions of twenty and even thirty years ago. While interest rates have reacted and are high, the amount required for down payments is still low. It is possible today to buy a house with absolutely nothing down and no credit. (See Chapter 5 for details.) In the future, to prevent speculation, the down-payment requirements will undoubtedly be raised, but for now it is still possible to gain extraordinarily high leverage in real estate.

3. Choose your investments to coincide with your security.

In today's modern recession selective unemployment is high and the threat of layoffs hangs over many individuals. There are, however, certain groups which are immune to unemployment—those on fixed incomes. Mainly pensioners and retirees, they comprise nearly 20 percent of the population. Regardless of how the economy declines, they will not be fired or laid off. Yet this exceptionally stable group of people is being threatened by inflation in real estate. Because their income is relatively fixed (it does go up, but usually much slower than inflation), they cannot afford the new houses and new apartments which are being built. (It is hard to live on less than $400 a month total income today.) This group provides a ready market for anyone who can offer good housing at prices its members want to pay. This may mean investing in such areas as trailer parks or in middle-aged apartment houses and renovating them, but by catering to this market it is possible to obtain a virtually vacancy-free income property that can recession-proof (even depression-proof) your future and make you an enormous profit when you sell.

These three guidelines coupled with average luck and common sense are what are needed to make big profits in real estate today.

They are purposely described in brief to make them easy to refer back to. Now on to using them.

The story of Gail and Howard VanTill in the next chapter is not unique. It is possible for anyone, young or old, married or single, with or without children to do what they did. The final requirement is determination.

The reader should note that while the following story of Howard and Gail is true and the investment histories of all other real and imaginary persons in this book are possible, they may not be repeated or duplicated by anyone else. Remember, there are *no guarantees* of success in any investment.

2

How to Make Large Profits in Real Estate Today— the Home Reinvestment Method

Here is the method that an average person can use to make large profits in real estate today. I call it the Home Reinvestment Plan. It involves the least risk when the investor is least experienced and yet allows the investor to increase the risk as he gains practical knowledge in buying and selling real estate.

A word about risk is in order here. Anytime you invest money there is a risk. *There are no sure things.* Investing in real estate, however, can reduce the risk to a point where it becomes as close to a sure thing as you can ever get. Making a fortune in real estate is much like the old game of Monopoly, which was in fact fashioned after the acquiring of real estate in Atlantic City. The game involves using a relatively small income to buy property, rent it out, sell it for profit, and buy more property. The process has been given various names such as "pyramiding your money" and, a more descriptive term, "reinvesting your profits." If we were playing at the crap tables in Las Vegas, it might be called "letting your bet ride."

This brings us back to the *game* aspect of making a fortune in real estate. Just as in the game of Monopoly you can lose, so too in real estate can you lose.

By using the Home Reinvestment Plan, however, you begin with the absolute smallest risk possible—no more risk than buying your own home. Then, as your expertise in the manipulation of property grows, it is possible to take greater risks for more profits. To illustrate how the Home Reinvestment Plan works, we shall take the case of a Los Angeles couple who have increased their capital from an initial $1,500 investment to more than $230,000 in less than six years!

Turning $1,500 into $230,000

When Gail and Howard VanTill were first married, they determined to make their fortune in real estate. They had no plan in mind but did have average luck coupled with extraordinary good sense. Their determination was the catalyst which, when added to their luck and good sense, made their success possible. They began by first assessing what they had to work with and then deciding how to use it to their best advantage to help them toward the goal of becoming wealthy.

Both Howard and Gail agreed that Gail would not work, so they would only have one income to apply toward their goal. Howard was a draftsman with a large electronics-aerospace industry, a moderate-risk job (in terms of employment possibilities) today; but assuming his plant did not lose too many government contracts and lay him off, he could count on a steady income which would rise, helping to keep up with inflation. In terms of 1975 dollars his income was $13,000 a year.

Gail wanted to have children but was willing to wait a few years to make their real estate fortune dream come true. Finally, they had $1,500 in cash from precious savings and wedding presents to work with.

They decided that the best way for them to get started was to buy a house to live in. If they chose wisely, they could sell for a profit. If they made a mistake, they could always live permanently in the house. As long as Howard's income continued, there was virtually no chance they could lose money in real estate this way.

Location, location, location!

Buying their first investment home was a big experience for Gail and Howard. They decided to pick the very best possible area for what they could afford, reasoning that the better the area, the better their chances when it came time to resell. Since they only had a total of $1,500 in savings and since Howard's income would not allow them to qualify for a very large loan, they chose Van Nuys, a moderate-income area in the San Fernando Valley of Los Angeles. The house they finally picked was in fairly good condition, but was priced less than others around it because it only had one bathroom instead of the usual two for the area. (It had three bedrooms.) Here is how they decided on this particular piece of property on Cherry Street.

They found the house through a Realtor®, a broker member of the National Association of Realtors (not all brokers are Realtors; there is a difference). He pointed out that while this house cost only $24,000, those nearby that were similar to it but had two bathrooms had sold recently for $26,000 to $27,000. They thanked the broker, went back to their apartment, and then called nearly a half-dozen other brokers specifically asking for a *two*-bath house in that area. Several were for sale, the lowest-priced at $26,500. They had confirmed what the broker had told them.

Next, by themselves, they went back and carefully looked over every *front yard* in the neighborhood. They were looking for old bottles and trash of any kind on the lawns, high weeds or unkept shrubs, and, particularly, old cars that were permanently parked on driveways with indications they were being worked on. (Heavy, large oil and grease stains in a driveway are sure signs that a car is worked on there regularly.) They decided that the way the neighborhood yards were kept was the first consideration in the buying and the reselling of a home in a moderate-income neighborhood.

Most of the homes on the block were well kept. Two, they noticed, had unusually extensive landscaping. One, on the other side of the street and two houses down, was moderately landscaped, the shrubs were overgrown, and the lawn was desperately in need of cutting. However, there was no trash on the lawn or oil stains in the driveway.

Next Gail went to the neighbors on both sides, introduced herself as a potential buyer of the house next door, and asked how far away was the nearest shopping, how convenient were the schools, and, more important, how were the other neighbors. Both neighbors seemed pleasant and gave favorable answers.

"Sometimes it's not important what you decide as long as you make a decision." GEN. DOUGLAS MACARTHUR

Last, the VanTills arranged to see the house a second time. Inside it was in fair condition. The paint was old and scratched in some places, but adequate. The stove and oven were usable but heavily greased. The back yard was overgrown with weeds. They took particular note of the fact that the current owner had recently recarpeted most of the house with carpeting of fairly good quality. Now they wrote down their impressions of the house pro and con.

PRO:
1. Good neighborhood
2. Good carpeting (probably the single item that makes the greatest impression when it comes to selling a house)
3. Good price
4. No repairs requiring a contractor's work
5. Almost no risk (if things did not work out, they could always live in the house for a few years)

CON:
1. Only one bathroom in a two-bathroom area
2. Poor to fair condition
3. Back yard undeveloped

The reader may think that other considerations should be taken account of. For example, how did they like the layout of the house, and were the colors appealing? How far from work was it for Howard? (It turned out to be 27 miles one way—far, but not unmanageable.) Did it have a workshop in the garage where he could putter? (It did.) These and other such questions are in fact what they should have considered if they had been buying the house to live in for pleasure. But they were buying the house to live in for *investment*.

For Gail and Howard, the main thing wrong was the single bathroom. They had to somehow get around this deficiency. They had no intentions of putting in a new bathroom, because of the cost, but they figured that only one bath would reduce the number of potential buyers at resale time. They reasoned, however, that it would not eliminate them all. It would be possible for them to sell for a higher price to someone who liked the area but did not mind a single bath— particularly if the house were fixed up.

The poor condition of the interior and yard did not bother them either. That was what they hoped would keep the price down to them. However, this is not what they told their Realtor.

They called the broker to their apartment and told him they wanted to make the following offer:

Price	$24,000 (full price)
Down payment	$1,350 (minimum down FHA at that time)
Balance	$22,650 (an FHA loan for the entire balance)
Closing costs	$150 (Approx. Seller was to pay all costs excluding impounds, which the buyers were required to pay.)

The broker had a smile on his face until the conditions were all brought out. Then he frowned and pointed out some reasons that the seller might not accept such an offer. He said the seller was already committed to paying the following costs:

Commission	$1,440 (6 percent of $24,000)
His own closing costs	$500 (roughly)
Total	$1,940

If he were to sell FHA, he would have to pay over $1,200 more because the "points," or discount rate (discussed in Chapter 5 on borrowing), were so high. And to pay the buyers' closing costs would add another point plus about $300 in closing costs, or $550 more. Following are additional costs *to seller:*

FHA points for seller	$1,200
FHA points buyer usually paid	$240
Buyers' closing costs	$300 (estimated)
Total additional costs	$1,740

The broker pointed out that since the house was already proportionally reduced because of the single bathroom, they were in effect asking the owner to drop his price about 7 percent below market value.

Howard agreed, then pointed out that both the yard and the house needed work. More importantly, he added, by selling FHA, even though he was not getting as much money as he wanted, the seller would be getting all cash. He would not need to take back any second loans himself.

The broker said that frankly, he did not think the seller would take it, but he was willing to try. A deposit receipt was drawn up and the broker left. Howard and Gail waited anxiously. A few hours later the broker called back saying their offer had been accepted; however, there was one minor change the seller wanted, and he (the broker) would be right over to get their initials on it.

Now the most difficult part of the negotiations began. When the broker arrived, he said the seller had agreed to all the conditions except those regarding the closing costs. He wanted the buyers to pay their normal costs.

Howard and Gail had discussed their response earlier. The house was only worth it if their initial investment could be low. Since they had very little cash, every extra cent they put in would be less they could use to fix up the place and less they would make in profit on a future sale. If they could not get the house at the agreed-upon price, they would find another, and this they told the broker.

He frowned and said it would cost them the deal. They replied that either the seller accepted the exact first offer or they would refuse to buy. Since the seller was easily reached, they gave the broker only one day to get his approval. The broker sighed and left saying they had just lost the house.

The seller signed.

"I saw it, but do I know what I saw?" Visitor to Cape Canaveral during takeoff of first manned space vehicle

This first purchase by Gail and Howard illustrates many important things to look for and points out those critical psychological moments when you get a deal that is either to your advantage or to someone else's.

The most important consideration Gail and Howard gave to location. They reasoned that regardless of what they did to improve the house they bought, if it was in a poor area, they would not be able to even get prospective buyers in the door to look at it. This could force them to reduce their price and give their house away as a "bargain" in order to induce buyers to come and check it out.

Second, they carefully chose a house that was well within what they guessed were their limits as far as fixing it up was concerned. No major construction work, but a lot of hard work at gardening and painting.

Third, they arranged the financing so that it was entirely to their advantage. Their reason for insisting on an FHA loan will be pointed out shortly. (While some sellers resign themselves to having to pay the higher costs of selling FHA, many, because they feel their house is fairly priced, are reluctant to do so. It is here that the broker earns his commission in convincing the seller to take less than he had hoped for in order to make a quick sale. Try never to be the seller in such a situation.)

Fourth, they had made up their minds what they were willing to pay and were not willing to budge. This is the single most critical aspect in buying real estate for investment. *Never* let your heart sway your mind. Set a price and conditions and stick to them. It is amazing how many times the people you are dealing with will back down in order to make a sale.

The supreme importance of elbow grease

With the purchase completed, Gail and Howard were anxious to begin making money on their real estate. They moved in and, using Howard's income, gradually did those things necessary to make the house salable at a higher figure. Gail wallpapered one wall in each of the rooms including the bathroom with striking paper, while Howard put in a back lawn and planted some inexpensive, leafy shrubs.

Some cleaning to the stove and oven, a shampooing of the carpet, and they were done. Then Howard walked across the street to the house that was in poor shape and offered to cut the lawn and trim the shrubs for 50 cents. Rather than be insulting by saying he was doing it because the appearance dragged down the neighborhood, he said he was doing it for exercise. The neighbor happily agreed.

The big test—was it all worth it?

Six months after they bought the house, after spending one day on weekends and several nights during each week (and Gail put in several days during each week), they were ready. They put their house up for sale at $28,000 *by owner*. They felt they would not need a broker because they expected a quick sale. They were right.

Why? It was the financing. Here is how it worked:

Howard knew that all modern FHA loans are completely assumable. That meant that the new buyers *did not have to qualify* as Howard did. They did not have to have good credit or even any money down. All they had to do was sign the assumption papers. (See Chapter 5.)

Howard and Gail put an advertisement in the *Valley Green Sheet*, a local paper well read for its housing advertisements. It read:

"Super area—good price for the right person—only $1,000 total down on a $28,000 house! NO QUALIFYING."

They had immediate responses; however, before even showing their house they carefully screened their prospective buyers. While the buyers did not have to qualify for the FHA loan, they had to have good enough credit to qualify for the *second mortgage* that Gail and Howard were going to loan them. That required making enough money to pay back both loans, a good steady job, and fairly good credit.

The VanTills had plans for that second loan, for it would be much like a valuable possession such as a car. But to make it salable either as an item to trade or to dispose of for cash, it had to be properly "aged"—it had to show a record of the mortgagor making his payments on time.

Three people in the first week seemed to meet the criteria, and they were shown the house. One couple wanted to buy. Gail got the couple's permission to run a credit check. Armed with the permission note, she went to a local credit agency, where for $12.50 she received a complete credit history on the couple. It disclosed that they had defaulted on two cars in the past three years, the husband frequently switched jobs, and they had a poor credit rating from the local stores. Gail and Howard refused to sell to them because of the findings.

Three weeks and a few prospective buyers later a couple turned up that seemed to have all the qualifications. The husband made in salary 3½ times the monthly payments on both loans, had held his job for three years, and was in a field—he was an auto mechanic—that promised a good future. The following sale was made:

Price	$28,000
Down payment	$1,000
First loan FHA	$23,000 (approx.)
Second loan	$4,000 (note to Gail and Howard)
Closing costs	Buyers and sellers each paid their normal costs

Since there were no loan points or commission involved, the only closing cost to Gail and Howard was the policy of title insurance. The buyers paid back to Gail and Howard the amount of money in the impound account (money Gail and Howard had advanced to pay for taxes and fire insurance) and the escrow fees.

For the buyers it was a good deal. They could not themselves qualify for an FHA loan (their income had to be at least four times the monthly loan plus insurance and taxes), they did not have the extra down payment it would take to purchase FHA, and they got a "doll house"—a term used frequently to describe a home in perfect condition.

It was a great deal for Gail and Howard. They had two-thirds of the original $1,500 back in cash and a $4,000 note that was to prove the start of their fortune.

Archimedes said, "With a lever long enough I could move the world." A small buyer with a lot of leverage can purchase a very big house.

Things moved faster after this.

One might have expected the VanTills would look around in the same neighborhood for a similar deal. They did not. Prior to selling their first house, they began looking for a new home in Brentwood, an exclusive section of Los Angeles where houses had been individually built over a thirty-year period, a cheap house might sell for $60,000 to $70,000, and $250,000 was not a unique price. For a month and a half they went out with every Realtor in the area, stopped at every "For Sale by Owner" sign, checked out every newspaper advertisement. (They rented for several months giving their second mortgage a chance to "age".) Finally they found what they wanted.

"A boulder blocked the roadway and the townspeople continually

bumped into it. Finally a stranger stopped and moved it away. It was gold." OLD CHINESE PROVERB

Two elderly sisters were selling their small three-bedroom house on Milnor Street which they owned free and clear. But the house had one decided drawback—it was slipping down a hill. The sisters had tried to get $60,000 for the home through a broker, but because of the slide had finally reduced their price to $40,000, where it now stood. They were selling "by owner."

Howard asked if he could have a soil report made. They agreed. Howard had a structural engineer–contractor look at the house at the same time. The soil report revealed that much slippage had occurred, and future slippage was possible unless severe corrective measures were taken. The house was tilted at an angle so that if you dropped a marble at one corner of the living room, it would immediately roll across the floor to the other end. But it was on a slab (a solid sheet of concrete) over 8 inches thick which had not broken. They decided to buy.

Gail and Howard had chosen Brentwood for three reasons. First, they figured that the potential for making a profit here would be greatest. If they could make $4,000 on a $25,000 house, or roughly 15 percent, they should be able to make the same 15 percent on a $60,000 house, but now the actual cash would be almost $10,000 (figuring a sales price of $70,000). Second, they thought that in an area such as Brentwood, which had houses built over the past thirty years, their chances for finding a home for investment that was greatly underpriced because of some unusual circumstances (such as a slide) was the greatest. Third, and most important, *Brentwood was not a tract area*. Each house tended to be unique, and it was difficult to compare the price of one home with another. Here they could sell for significantly more than they paid.

Their pro and con sheet looked like this:

PRO:
1. Excellent neighborhood
2. Excellent price

CON:
1. Severe problem with slippage
2. Poor or inadequate carpeting (remember, the single most impressive item in a house)
3. House in fair condition, yard in fair condition

The difference between this assessment and the one for the house on Cherry Street was that this house was closer to Howard's work (only 13 miles away), it did require contractor's work, and it had an element of risk. As we shall see from the VanTills' offer, if things did not work out, they could not "sit on" the house and live in it. However, now they were working with someone else's money (the $4,000 second loan), and they felt it time to take a chance.

They purchased the Milnor Street home, and the figures looked like this:

Price	$40,000
Down payment	$1,000 cash plus the $4,000 second note from the Cherry Street property
First loan	$35,000 to be held by the sisters for one year only, then to be paid off in cash (the sisters agreed to subordinate this first loan to a construction loan of no more than $10,000)
Closing costs	$300

The sellers went along with the offer because of the unusual loan arrangement. They knew that no lending institution would make a loan on a house that was falling down the hill, and they were reconciled to having to carry the loan themselves. The VanTills' offer guaranteed that they would only have to carry the loan for one year (at 10 percent interest, by the way), and then they would get cash. Subordinating (making their loan come second in the event of foreclosure to a construction loan) did not bother them because the amount of the construction loan was specified and was relatively low.

The VanTills' calculated that they would be able to correct the house's unique problem within one year and then either sell at a profit or refinance. There lay the risk. If they could not complete the correction, the two nice old sisters would foreclose and take the property back.

When you don't know, ask someone.

The structural engineer who had appraised the situation before the purchase told Howard that the house could be righted and maintained level by sinking a piling at one corner. Then earth could be filled in underneath and foliage planted on the hill to prevent future erosion. Including the city permit, subcontracting, and steel reinforcing, the whole job should not run over $7,000.

Immediately after the purchase Howard went to the bank he did business with and asked for a construction loan. The bank would advance the VanTills money to have the structural work done in exchange for a first mortgage on the home. Remember, the sisters agreed to subordinate their loan. After examining the structural engineer's report, the bank agreed, but insisted on paying out the money only as the work was completed.

The construction crew came and sank a 15-foot piling into the ground at one corner of the house and then, using this as a foundation, jacked the house up until it was level. Then earth was packed in underneath, and finally Howard planted the hillside to prevent future erosion. Cost: $9,000. Howard had learned a lesson here; appraisals of work to be done are *almost always* less than the actual cost. Fortunately, he had allowed himself some margin by requesting a $10,000 loan and was covered.

Gail had the floors sanded and polished at a cost of $600 and then left them bare. They were oak and, although not carpeted, gave the house an elegant feel. Of course she also painted, and added wallpaper to one wall of each room, a feature that was to become a trademark of the houses she and Howard owned. After seven months they put their house up for sale by owner.

They got a buyer within two months for $70,000.

What to one person appears to be sheer luck may in reality be another's careful planning.

Their asking price was $75,000, not an unreasonable price for a "doll house" in such an area. (The sisters had originally wanted $60,000. Add to this 15 percent, or $9,000, for fix-up plus $5,000 to $6,000 to bargain with and you get the price.) But before putting the house on the market, Howard had gone to a local savings and loan, told them how much he was planning to sell for, and asked them for a "loan commitment." Without cost to him the savings and loan appraiser came out, and on his recommendation the savings and loan agreed to loan 80 percent of the *selling price*. The appraiser felt that the area had many unique houses. If the VanTills could find someone willing to pay $75,000 and put 20 percent down, then the house was undoubtedly worth that much. Armed with this information, Howard pointed out to each prospective buyer that a well-known savings and loan in the area agreed to loan 80 percent of $75,000—a convincing argument to prove value.

The deal they finally made read as follows:

Selling price	$70,000
Down by buyer	$15,000
First loan	$55,000

It was a straightforward deal with the buyers paying cash down to a new loan. For them it was good because this was an elegant house in an elegant neighborhood. For Howard and Gail it was again an excellent deal. Their profit and loss sheet looked like this:

Purchase price	$40,000
Improvement loan	10,000
Total	$50,000
Selling price	$70,000
Profit	$20,000 (on a $5,000 investment)

Since the federal government allows persons to defer gains realized on the sale of a home as long as the money is reinvested in another home within one year and as long as the new purchase price is higher, there were no federal taxes to pay.

If you can't have fun at what you're doing, it's probably not worth doing.

The VanTills' next house was also in Brentwood. It cost them $72,000 and was unique among the houses they owned. It was a castle!

Purchase price	$72,000
Down payment	$15,000
First loan	$57,000

They had been able to obtain roughly a 75 percent loan from a bank, much more than Howard would normally qualify for with his salary, because of their excellent "track record"—successful experience in the market they were in—and because the bank appraiser had noted that this house on Justin Street could easily be worth twice the purchase price if it was in "doll house" shape. However, it had been on the market for over a year, and no one had been willing to tackle its run-down condition until now.

This was the first house that the VanTills had bought that was very run down. In addition to the problems of fixing up broken plaster, windows, holes in the roof, etc., they had the problem of making payments on an enormous first loan as well as on the taxes, which were $1,800 a year, or $150 a month. But they had Howard's regular income plus some cash profit from their last sale to fall back on. Besides, it was getting to be great fun, and they had never imagined they would be living in such an extraordinary house. Their pro and con sheet looked like this:

PRO:
1. Excellent neighborhood
2. Good price
3. Good potential for doubling the value due to poor condition

CON:
1. Very poor condition
2. Some good but old carpeting (many tile floors)
3. Financing and taxes that were over their heads

Again the VanTills were purchasing a piece of property with a higher risk factor. They could not hope to make the monthly loan payments, which worked out to roughly $600 per month, plus the taxes of $150 a month, on Howard's salary. However, they had set aside a little of their profit on Milnor Street, and they thought they could carry along for perhaps a year and a half. If after that time they had not completely refurbished the home, they would be forced to sell for whatever they could get because they would not be able to continue making the payments. But they were bolstered by their recent success. They had learned that they could accomplish more than they had ever dreamed possible, simply by starting small and building on their experience. Besides, they were still working with someone else's money, and this house carried less immediate risk than their last purchase. If their time ran out, they could always sell at a loss here. If time had run out on their last property, they would simply have lost it. Success gave them confidence, and common sense made them realize that while this house was a bit risky, given average luck it was not above their heads.

The house had been built in the late thirties by a film producer and had seven bedrooms and five bathrooms, not to mention a huge living room, dining room, and gaming room. It was a place that would be fun to fix.

Here's how they did it.

They arranged an improvement loan from their bank for $10,000, the money to be paid out as improvements were made and they proceeded. It was simply a case of modernizing. They replaced all the old bathroom fixtures, completely modernized the kitchen, repainted and wallpapered as usual, trimmed and replanted in the yard, replaced broken windows, and in general did everything necessary to make the place elegant. Howard had to borrow another $5,000 before they were finished. It took over a year. By now they were not spending all their evenings and weekends working. They were taking time out to enjoy and entertain in their magnificent home.

One year and one month later they sold for $177,000.

The buyer turned out to be a plastic surgeon who liked being able to say that a movie producer had designed and built his home. Here again the uniqueness of the house is what brought "top dollar." In selling, the VanTills advertised that there was not another "mansion" like it in Los Angeles. They played up both the nostalgia of an older home and the modernization they had done. The buyer was happy with the price, and his lawyers arranged financing for him so that Gail and Howard again received cash.

Their profit and loss sheet looked like this:

Paid	$72,000
Improvement loans	$15,000
Profit used to offset loan and taxes (in addition to Howard's salary)	($5,000)
Total	$87,000
Selling price	$177,000
Profit	$90,000 (on a $15,000 investment)

"Money is like an arm and leg—use it or lose it." HENRY FORD

Now Gail and Howard had to make a decision. As they progressed to higher and higher priced homes, they were faced with the problem of greatly reduced numbers of potential buyers. For every 1,000 buyers for a $25,000 home, there were probably only half a dozen for a $250,000 home. In addition, in order for the VanTills to keep deferring payments of income taxes on their profits, each house they bought had to be *higher* in price than the preceding one, after expenses. Since they were already at the $177,000 level, this could soon become a major stumbling block.

They could have, of course, continued slowly buying more expensive houses and selling them for greater profits; however, they realized that because of diminished numbers of buyers and the tax problem, their risk was greater than before. Faced with an increased risk, they decided to look into other areas to find out what else was available. Their first choice was an apartment building. Here they felt they could at least avoid the problem of fewer buyers (regardless of the price at selling time), and, they soon learned, they also could continue to defer their taxes.

Adding the Income Reinvestment method to the Home Reinvestment method

For the VanTills purchasing an apartment building was somewhat like jumping into a pool of ice-cold water. They were pretty sure they would be all right once inside, but they were afraid of that first shock when they would find out just how cold it was. Thus far in their career in real estate investment they had bought only houses, in which they themselves lived. They had never in their lives rented an apartment to someone else. They were not sure what a tenant would demand and need, they were uncertain about what they could do if a tenant failed to pay rent, and finally they were most unsure of what kind of an apartment building to purchase.

They chose to buy an apartment house because it was in the field most similar to the one they had experience in. Apartments, after all, are just a grouping of small houses all clumped together, or so they reasoned. They realized, however, that their past experience was solefully lacking when it came to knowledge of what a *good* apartment investment was. They understood that in a sense they were starting over and that as novices in a large investment they probably faced greater chances of losing their money than at any time before in their real estate investment career. But they also knew that they had risked their money before and that by using common sense and expecting average luck they had always made a profit. Unless they did something very foolish or were very unlucky, the chances were that they would come out on top again. Also, they realized that the potential for profit with an apartment building should be much greater than with a house, and this tended to balance out the risk.

"In business, either you're moving forward or you're falling behind, but you're never standing still." CORNELIUS VANDERBILT

They started the same way they had with their first home purchase. They reasoned out what would be the best buy for them. (It is amazing how far a person can get on common sense alone.) They realized that they were in the midst of a modern recession, that in certain types of occupations unemployment was high, and that in addition there was a chronically high rate of inflation. They reasoned that the safest apartment investment they could make would be in a building with fairly low rents. Presumably, there are *always* people available as tenants as you *decrease* the rental cost regardless of unemployment. But in times of high inflation there would undoubtedly be an even greater number of people available whose incomes had not kept pace with rising costs. They would be actively seeking lower-cost housing.

Of course, the VanTills had no intention of buying a tenement, the lowest-cost housing there is. Howard had done some research at the library and discovered that tenements were based on the principle of getting as many people into a given amount of living space as possible. The theory went something like this. Say you can rent three rooms out to one family for $100. If you can cram three families into the same rooms by offering them rents of only $50, you can increase your return by 50 percent, renting for a total of $150. Unfortunately, it is usually only the very poor, who cannot possibly afford more than $50, who are forced to live in such conditions. Howard was astonished to learn that the great tenement buildings that exist today in

New York are not run-down apartment buildings that once saw better days. These buildings *were designed* as tenements. They were constructed to have an occupancy of anywhere from two to ten people per room, with provisions for toilets and kitchens limited to one or two per floor. New York, in fact, had the country's worst slums in the 1870s. A hundred years ago politicians and reformers spoke in glowing terms of the next century (this one) when the tenements would finally come down.

The VanTills chose to look in North Hollywood. Geographically it was one of the sections of the central city that was still fairly young, having been built up some fifteen to twenty years ago. It was a moderately priced area and not run down. It was almost as far from Howard's work as their first investment house on Cherry Street.

After contacting a number of Realtors and looking at half a dozen buildings, they found the apartment house on Waverly Street. It contained thirty units. It was fairly modern but needed paint and fixing up. The biggest problem Gail and Howard saw was the number of units. They had never rented out an apartment before, and here they were considering buying thirty of them!

"No man acquires property without acquiring with it a little arithmetic, also."　EMERSON

Here is how they decided on the Waverly Street apartments. First they looked at the income and expense sheet the owner provided them. They were particularly concerned with income.
Income on Waverly Street:

All two-bedroom units with kitchens and single baths—thirty units
All rented for $135 per month (*thirty-day leases only*)

Monthly income	$ 4,050
Yearly income	$48,600
Less 5% vacancy	$ 2,430
Total annual income	$46,170

The owner stated a vacancy rate of only 5 percent. This seemed strangely low to the VanTills, particularly since there were two vacancies, or nearly 7 percent, at the present time. Also, they had heard stories of apartment buildings with vacancies as high as 25 percent.

They asked their Realtor, and he indicated that apartments in this area of town normally had vacancy factors of about 5 percent. They called two other Realtors, who confirmed this statement. Still unsatisfied, they knocked on the doors of several tenants and talked to two who had been in the building for three and seven years, respectively. The first said that people hardly ever came and went. The two vacancies at the time were unusual as most of the time the place was full. The second and older tenant confirmed what the first had said. The VanTills were skeptical, but willing to accept the 5 percent figure for the moment.

Next they looked at the owner's expense sheet. Listed were items under his payments for his loans. They paid no attention to these, as they expected to get new financing. They instead checked those figures which were ones they would have to pay.

Expense sheet on Waverly property:

Property taxes	$14,000 annually
Maintenance	Owner did this himself.
Repairs	$1,200 annually
Management	Owner did this himself.

Common sense told them that the owner was painting an overly bright picture. There should be allowances for maintenance and management regardless of who performed the work, and $1,200 a year seemed very low for repairs on thirty units. They needed another opinion.

They scouted the area until they saw a comparable apartment building. It had twenty-six units. The owner lived there also and was willing to give them some information. He figured he spent $100 a year *per unit*, on the average, for work, including cleaning up after tenants moved out. Also, he pointed out that he had to advertise every time there was a vacancy and that this cost him $5 a month on the average, and his being there meant he did not get the rent from the apartment he occupied, which he figured as his management charge. Finally he paid for all the water and garbage collection, which worked out to about $100 *per unit per year*. He pointed out that since most of the units were rented to middle-aged to older couples without children, management was not too big a headache.

The VanTills drew up a new expense sheet:

Property taxes	$14,000 (including personal property tax on furniture, stoves, etc.)
Operational costs (utilities)	3,000 $100 per unit a year)
Repairs	3,000 ($100 per unit a year)
Management	1,500 (cost of one unit a year they would occupy)
Total	$21,500

One last and significant thing they found out from the second owner was that he was charging *$150 a month* for his two-bedroom units and also reported only a 5 percent vacancy factor.

The VanTills now considered the price. It was $276,000. The broker indicated it had been arrived at in this manner. A "cost factor" (see Chapter 3 for an additional explanation) of 6 had been used on the annual total income, multiplying by 6 to arrive at the current price. When the VanTills asked why 6 had been chosen, the broker indicated that it was an arbitrary figure. Cost factors from 5 to 7 were commonly used. A property such as this that was not in grade A condition but that had such a low vacancy factor deserved a factor of 6. A quick check of other brokers in the area established this as a true statement.

"Always be sure you know which side of the bread the butter's on."
W. C. FIELDS

Now the VanTills attempted to figure out what would be a good price for them. They accepted the cost factor of 6, but multiplied it by their own estimate of annual income:

Total (gross) income	$ 48,600
less	1,500 (for unit manager-occupied)
less	2,430 (5% vacancies)
Actual gross income	$ 44,670
	× 6 (cost factor)
	$268,020

The difference between their computation and the asking price was roughly $9,000. Now the VanTills figured what their loan cost would be. They were told that the owner would give them a loan for 75 percent of the value for twenty-five years, or roughly $201,000. This would mean monthly payments of $1,780 at 9 percent per year interest, or $20,360 per year. Their projected expenses would look something like this with one-fourth, or $67,000, down:

Expenses for one year:

Taxes	$14,000	
Loan costs	20,000	(roughly)
Operational cost	3,000	
Repairs	3,000	
Total	$40,000	
Income	$44,000	(approx.)
Profit	$ 4,000	

On a $67,000 investment they could hope only to get a return of roughly 5 percent on their money. While this was not particularly good for a real estate investment, the VanTills did not object. They knew the rents per apartment were at least $15 a month lower than in a comparable building and potentially could be raised to increase their income.

The picture became even brighter when Howard and Gail considered the tax angle. Here is what they could deduct the first year on their income taxes:

Property taxes	$14,000	
*A Interest on loan	30,000	(The seller would take the loan back himself and agreed to one year's prepaid interest.)
Operational cost	3,000	
Repairs	3,000	
B. Depreciation	12,500	
*C. Fix-up repairs	8,300	
Total deductions	$71,000	(rounded)

Now they considered the $44,000 in income they would receive the first year from the rents on Waverly Street and subtracted it from their deductible expenses.

Deductions	$71,000
Less income	44,000
Taxable *loss*	$27,000

Although they would actually be pocketing $4,000 in cash, for income tax purposes they would be losing $27,000. This not only meant they did not have to pay any tax on the $4,000; it also meant they could apply the $27,000 loss to their other income.

The item marked *A is prepaid interest. The government allows the owner of an apartment building to deduct all the interest he pays on his mortgages in the year he buys and the next year. Since Howard and Gail bought in January and the seller was willing to accept prepaid interest and Howard had enough from his $90,000 to pay both the down payment ($67,000) and the extra $15,000, he did so and took the deduction.

The item marked *B refers to depreciation. Owners of relatively new apartment buildings can often take an accelerated depreciation on them. Howard calculated the building was worth $200,000, or 75 percent of the selling price (based on the tax assessor's figures). He figured its life expectancy to be twenty years. (A recent government study revealed that the actual life expectancy of the average apartment building is between fifty and seventy-five years!) On a straight line from the first year to the twentieth the depreciation would be $10,000 per year. On an accelerated depreciation it would be 125 percent of $10,000, or $12,500 the first year. (See Chapter 8 on real estate tax problems for a further explanation.)

The item marked *C refers to the repairs to the building that Howard and Gail planned to make as soon as they took ownership. This included completely painting it inside and out and fixing broken doors, windows, and appliances, plus some landscaping. The government normally will allow *up to* 5 percent of the sales price for fixing up property, to be deducted in the first year. (As a rule of thumb, if more than 5 percent is spent or if the spending is on something other than repairs, the government normally assumes that it is part of an overall project to upgrade the building and requires that it be depreciated over five or more years.)

Now they considered their profits from a tax viewpoint (Table 2-1). Since they had held the house on Justin Street more than six months, the government would allow them to declare this profit as *capital gains*. This meant they would not have to pay regular tax on it. (Regular tax is simply the normal income tax paid at the end of the year which would have put them into the 60 percent tax bracket.)

In paying capital gains tax they declared only half their profit. In other words, $57,000 was not taxed. The remaining $57,000 was added to Howard's income. This was better, but it still could put them into a 50 percent tax bracket. (See Chapter 8 for an alternate method of figuring capital gains.)

Table 2-1 Tax Evaluation

Deferred profit on Cherry Street	$ 4,000
Deferred profit on Milnor Street	20,000
Profit on Justin Street	90,000
Total profit	$114,000
Less capital gains exclusion (one-half)	57,000
Taxable profit	$ 57,000
Howard's regular income	13,000
Total taxable income	$ 70,000
Waverly Street tax loss	27,000
Actual taxable income	$ 43,000
Actual tax (approximately after exemptions and itemized deductions including taxes and interest on the properties—$7,000)	$10,340
Less withholding	2,100
Tax yet to be paid	$ 8,240

However, if they purchased the apartment building on Waverly Street, they would show a first-year *loss* of $27,000 (see deductions just listed). Under current Internal Revenue Service (IRS) regulations, they could normally deduct this $27,000 from the $70,000 income reducing their total income to $43,000.

After withholding from Howard's job, their regular tax on this amount was roughly $9,000. (Howard knew, of course, that the money he did not have to pay in taxes was only deferred, that is, put off until a future date.) However, their actual cash back from Justin Street was ten times this amount!

First loan	$ 57,000
Improvement Loans	15,000
Total Loans	$ 72,000
Cash from sale	177,000
Cash left after paying loans	$105,000

Lest the reader who is new to tax shelters think Howard's actions were not entirely on the level, he is referred to Chapter 8 where tax shelters on apartment houses are explained in more detail.

"Nothing seems so complicated as what one doesn't know—nothing so simple as what one understands." JOHN DEWEY

The incentive for Howard and Gail to buy was there. Besides, they had a plan which, if it worked, would increase their money dramatically on the resale in a fairly short time. They knew that the price was determined by the income of the building. It was six times whatever the total, or *gross amount*, realized from rents would be. They also knew that the building was renting for less than others in the area. If they bought, fixed up, and eventually *raised* rents, they would increase their gross income. When it came time to sell, they would be able to multiply the 6 by a higher income figure than when they bought, giving them a higher sales price and a profit. (If the rents, for example, are $100 a year, then the selling price is arrived at by multiplying $100 by 6, which gives $600. If, however, the rent is raised by only $10, the selling price is now $110 times 6, or $660. Every $1 *per year* increase in rents is worth $6 when it comes time to sell. Every $1 *per month* increase in rent is worth $72 when it comes time to sell.)

Their pro and con sheet looked like this:

PRO:
1. The potential of dramatic profits when they sold by increasing rents
2. An enormous savings on their tax liability on the profit of Justin Street

CON:
1. Their total inexperience in the field of apartment-house management
2. The headache that was bound to come from handling thirty units
3. The chance of losing all their money

Howard reduced the con side by agreeing to take a course in property management from a large realty company in the area. (The local adult school had a similar program.) Gail pointed out that they were basically working with someone else's money. If they lost it, they could always start over.

They made an offer of $267,000, one-fourth down and the seller to take back the mortgage, allowing one year's prepayment of interest. Since the seller did not own the building free and clear but had a small $30,000 mortgage on it, he would have to pay off his mortgage and the real estate commission with the down payment and receive very little cash himself.

However, he was planning to retire, and the thought of $1,800 a month coming in on the loan without any rental headaches was appealing. Besides, he did have the extra money from the interest. He agreed to the offer. (He had not figured his tax advantages at all and at the end of the year had a real headache, but that is another story.)

Buyer's remorse and success!

The deal was made, but at the last minute, just as Howard and Gail were about to sign the final papers, they got "cold feet." They panicked and wanted out at all costs. What did they know about running a thirty-unit apartment building? What if they actually lost the $90,000? Could they really build it up again?

Their fears are commonly known as "buyers' remorse." This is a psychological condition that attacks virtually all buyers. It is a mental process of having second thoughts that comes with accepting the facts of what you have done financially. Howard and Gail cried a little, laughed a little, and went ahead. They were worried about what they had to lose; but if they were successful . . .?

As soon as the deal went through and the closing costs were paid and occupancy was turned over to them, Howard and Gail moved into the former owner's now-vacant apartment. Then they went from door to door and introduced themselves to all the tenants.

They found that most were congenial and openly accepted them. A few expressed regret over the change of ownership. The VanTills informed each tenant that they planned certain "renewal" work which would begin soon on the apartment building. The tour not only introduced them to the tenants but also gave them an opportunity to inspect each apartment. Most were in good shape, kept so by the occupants; a few were badly in need of paint. The tenants who complained of deteriorating paint or torn carpets or appliances that did not work were assured that everything would be corrected soon.

Within a month, the VanTills had arranged for the complete painting of the outside of the building as well as whatever interior work the tenants requested. (Remember, they had more than $8,000 set aside for this.) In several cases they bought new air conditioners; they bought a new stove for one tenant, and they installed a new sink for another. A few months later they had all walkways finished and had placed new shrubs in boxes both on the second-floor walkways, which were open to the outside, and in a courtyard around which the building was constructed. In general relying on their past experience in homes, they spent a year turning the apartment building into a "doll house." The immediate cost was the $8,300 they had provided for from the remains of their profit on the Justin Street property. This gave them the $4,000 profit on the rentals that year to spend on themselves.

The VanTills' particular concern was the vacant apartments. These were completely repainted, carpeted, and wallpapered. After a few weeks the original two vacancies had been readied, and in the local paper they advertised a two-bedroom apartment for rent for $155. The area was close in, the apartments were fixed up beautifully, and the other tenants, being almost entirely without children, were quiet. And the rentals were among the cheapest rentals in the area. The two vacancies were quickly filled.

Selecting tenants: The rental agreement

In showing vacancies Gail would point out the advantages of cleanliness, location, and so on, while subtly questioning prospective tenants about their pets and children. They were willing to take one child if the child seemed quiet and a dog or cat if it seemed well controlled. They were looking primarily for middle-aged tenants. If after a time Gail was satisfied with the potential tenants and they expressed interest in the apartment, she would simply say, "I doubt that you can do better for this price anywhere in town. Shall I draw up a rental agreement?" It may seem simple, but in order to rent apartments it is almost always necessary to say that. The prospective tenants will usually take a short while to consider and then refuse or agree to rent.

Howard and Gail's rental agreement was relatively simple. It noted the names and former addresses of the tenants, their occupations, and their places of employment. It asked for several credit references, bank references, and permission to make a credit inquiry. In addition it specified the number of persons and pets that would occupy the apartment, the exact rent, the day the rent was due, and the place it was to be paid and said that the tenancy was "month to month"— either party could terminate it upon thirty days written notice.

The rental agreement specified that if for any reason the tenant failed to pay the rent on the due date, the tenancy was ended and he or she agreed to vacate the premises at the discretion of the owners. The agreement also included provisions for penalties if the rent was not paid and the premises were not vacated. And finally, the tenants had to agree to pay any and all legal costs if an eviction proceeding had to be started.

Most of the language of the agreement was designed to simply inform the tenant of what the owners expected of him, since the procedures for eviction were already carefully outlined in state and city codes (an explanation of which Howard received by consulting a local attorney, who also checked the VanTills' rental agreement).

"Speak softly but carry a big stick."   THEODORE ROOSEVELT

During the year they had only one bad experience with tenants, a couple named Forgeman. It turned out that the former owner had hedged a bit when he said that all the tenants were paid up in their rents. The Forgemans were actually three months behind. They paid usually within two weeks of the due date, but each time Howard went to collect they grumbled about the paint or the plumbing or the heating or some other feature of their apartment. Howard and Gail repainted their entire apartment and had the heating and plumbing systems checked (no trouble was found). Still the Forgemans refused to catch up with their back rent.

"Never ask a penny less than what's owed."   J. J. ASTOR

Since the back rent had really been due the former owner, Howard told the Forgemans he would make a deal with them. He would forget about collecting it, leaving that to the former owner, provided they would pay the current rent on the exact day it was due. The Forgemans were pleased with the arrangement (as well they should have been), and the first month the rent was paid promptly. The next month, however, it was three weeks late. Gail went to the Forgemans' apartment to find out if they were having financial difficulties. She was treated briskly by Mrs. Forgeman but was informed that Mr. Forgeman was regularly employed as a construction worker and made "very good money." Mrs. Forgeman said that the VanTills were lucky to have them as tenants. No children, no loud noises at night (this Gail knew was not entirely true), and no pets. Further, she said it was none of Gail's business how much money her husband made or how they spent it. Mrs. Forgeman ended, in a sort of threatening voice, "You know we are always good for the money, don't you dear?" Then she insisted Gail leave the apartment.

The next month the Forgemans were one week later on the rent. This, added to the three weeks the previous month, put them four weeks behind. When the following month they did not pay on the due date, Howard served them with a a three-day eviction notice. Either they had to pay up all back rents (two months rent, $270) or they had to move out.

Mrs. Forgeman was outraged, and that evening Mr. Forgeman stormed into Howard and Gail's apartment and noisily delivered the message that he and his wife would *neither pay nor move*. He said he considered the insult of an eviction notice worth at least a month's rent. When Howard disagreed, Mr. Forgeman left with this warning: "You just try and evict us. You'll find out what trouble is."

Three days later (allowing for the full term of the notice) Howard went to his attorney and started eviction proceedings. This cost him $150 to the attorney and $150 bond to the city, which carried out the eviction. It took a week. When the sheriff showed up to remove the Forgemans, they meekly asked for one more day. Howard relented. Within twenty-four hours they were gone, but not forgotten.

When Howard and Gail checked the apartment, they could not believe their eyes. The walls had been smeared with black paint, great quantities of which had also been dumped on the carpeting. The wall heater had been ripped from the wall and thrown on the floor. Fortunately a gas safety valve had operated, preventing any gas leakage. The sink in the kitchen had been cracked, as had the toilet in the bathroom. And all the loose parts from the stove were missing.

It took Howard and Gail two weeks and $500 to put the apartment back into shape, and they never got their back rent. This was all deductible from taxes, however, and offset by the increase in rents to $155 they received from this and the other apartments they rented. They had met their most severe initiation into the hazards of apartment house ownership.

"*Business is business.*"   OCTAVE MIRBEAU

After *one year*, the building was refurbished. Then Howard and Gail drew up a notice that they were increasing rents on *all* apartments to $165 per month within thirty days and dropped it in the mailbox of each tenant.

They knew they were lighting a potential powder keg, for the old tenants could conceivably revolt and move out. To head this off, the VanTills included a notice of a meeting they were planning to hold the following week where all tenants could express their views. The place was a nearby hall Howard and Gail rented for one night. Finally they indicated that any tenants who could not attend were cordially invited to come to the VanTills' apartment and express their views. Howard and Gail knew that calling a meeting of all the tenants was an extraordinary thing to do. However, Howard had read of the case of a large developer on the East Coast who planned to turn an apartment building into condominiums. He hoped to *sell* each tenant the apartment he or she was living in. In order to avoid angry repercussions by the tenants after he informed them of his intentions, he called a meeting where they could ask questions and lodge protests. Out of eighty tenants, only fifteen eventually refused to buy.

For a week things at Waverly Street were unusually quiet. Howard and Gail decided it would add prestige to their building if they gave it a name, so they called it Waverly Manor. They had a small gold sign with the name on it put up at the front of the building.

Toward the end of the week two tenants came to see the VanTills. They said they were on pensions and could not afford to pay $165 a month. The VanTills pointed out the improvements that had been made and the rising cost of living. They emphasized that comparable apartments were rented for much more than the $135 the original tenants were still paying and finished by saying they felt compelled to raise rents. Then they asked the tenants how much more they could afford. After considering, one admitted he could pay $150; the other, who met separately with the owners, said $145. The VanTills said they would consider and let each know after the meeting.

Nearly every tenant was there, and there was a charged and somewhat angry tenor to the crowd. The VanTills had provided coffee. They handed each tenant, as he or she walked in the door, a summary sheet. It noted all the improvements that had been made to the building since they arrived. In addition it contained a list of ten apartment buildings in the immediate area which contained two-bedroom units. The list pointed out that the most expensive in the area, a new building, rented such units for over $225 a month. The cheapest rented for $150 a month and was currently 100 percent occupied. Howard had done some homework.

Howard called the meeting to order and then read the summary sheet and commented on it. He said that he wanted them all to remain as tenants but that he felt justified in raising the rents. He noted that if there were any hardship cases they could see him privately, as two had already done, and these would be considered individually. Then he threw this meeting open to questions, answers, and general discussion.

"Careful planning, precise execution, a little luck—how can you lose?" A SERGEANT IN VIETNAM

For about an hour, the tenants voiced their anger at having the rents raised. Howard and Gail as calmly as possible repeated their justification. When a consortium of tenants insisted that no improvements had been done to their particular apartments, Howard and Gail agreed to repaint all apartments in the building that needed it over the next year and to fix or replace any defective items. They pointed out that they had already done such work for every tenant who had notified them of need.

The meeting lasted nearly three hours. As it concluded nothing seemed decided, on the surface. Howard and Gail had not backed down, but the tenants had not said they would not pay. It was in fact a great victory for the VanTills, as future events demonstrated.

The next day many of the tenants seemed friendlier, although a few remained aloof. The real test came one month later when the new rents were due. Five tenants moved out, Howard and Gail lowered the rents to $150 and $145 for the two tenants who had requested special treatment, and the rest paid $165. It took about a month to rent the vacant apartments, but eventually the building was filled up, and over the ensuing year the vacancy factor returned to a 5 percent average.

Howard and Gail retained ownership of Waverly Manor until June 1974. During their period of ownership they raised rents a second time, keeping up with the inflation of the modern recession. At the time they sold, they were *averaging* $175 a month per unit. Some were rented for less to hardship cases; others rented for $180.

The sales price was six times their gross annual income.

Monthly income	$ 5,075	(twenty-nine units at $175)
Annual income	60,900	
	× 6	
Selling price	$365,400	

Since they then owed $196,000 on their single loan, their equity was $169,400. They had almost doubled their money in two years.

A new kind of transaction, a new kind of property

If they sold for cash, Howard and Gail knew they would have the same problem with taxes they had had on the Justin Street house. All their equity would be considered profit. Even with the advantage of capital gains they would have to pay taxes on at least half of the nearly $170,000, or roughly $85,000.

Howard had done some studying, however, and had discovered that while taxes were applied to profit from a cash sale, no taxes were levied on an exchange of equities. If he could trade their apartment house for another piece of property, presumably one they could make a further profit on, they would not have to pay any taxes on the profit on Waverly Street. (The tax is not forgiven, just deferred until eventually a cash sale is made.)

There were two basic requirements for such a *tax-free exchange*, they discovered. First, the new property had to be of a "like kind." In Howard and Gail's case this simply meant it had to be income-producing property. It was doubtful, for example, that if they were to purchase a bowling-ball-manufacturing plant it would be considered "like kind." However, other apartments, a commercial building, or even a trailer park would. The second requirement was that there be no cash exchanged between the parties, or no "boot." This meant that the parties would exchange only their equities. They would have to find someone who wanted to trade who had at least a $170,000 equity, or interest, in a piece of property.

It took them nearly four months of looking to find what they wanted this time. It was actually two pieces of property a short distance north in Studio City, an area comparable to their present North Hollywood. Through a "For Sale by Owner" advertisement in the local shopping guide they found a Mr. Thomas who wanted to sell two pieces of property—his sixteen-unit apartment building *and* his sixty-pad trailer park.

Howard and Gail were familiar with *apartment buildings* by now, but had no experience with *trailer parks*. However, in checking with several brokers they found that the two were essentially the same type of operation. The sales price was usually six times the gross income. Management was normally less of a problem, since there were simply fewer things to go wrong. Expenses were roughly the same, but at tax time there was less to depreciate since no building was involved.

Howard learned from his accountant that he could depreciate the cement pads the trailers were on, the roadways, and the small clubhouse that was near the center of the park. What particularly interested the VanTills was the fact that the trailer pads were rented out for $40 a month and the owner showed no vacancy factors at all. After touring the park, Gail and Howard saw that indeed all the pads were rented. Later, when the deal was closer to completion, they went back and called on every tenant and asked to see receipts for the previous month's rent. In every case the tenant was either able to provide the receipt or an explanation for what had happened to it. (The VanTills had explained that they were purchasing the court and wanted to verify rental rates—the tenants cooperated fully.)

The receipts proved two points: (1) the rent was in fact $40 per month, and (2) every pad was indeed rented out, and the owner had not parked relatives and friends on them to make the lot appear full. Next the VanTills checked at other trailer parks in the area. They found rents ranged anywhere from $30 per month to $70 per month, depending on the condition of the park and how new it was. The *new* parks generally rented for much more—and had many vacancies.

Their pro and con sheet looked like this:

PRO:
1. Relatively low rents so the potential existed for raising them and making a dramatic profit at selling time
2. The possibility of exchanging properties so they would not have to pay taxes on Waverly Manor

CON:
1. Their inexperience with trailer parks
2. Many more rentals than they had handled previously

"Fear of the unknown is in the mind—you need only conquer it once to vanquish it forever." ISAAC BABEL

Once again Howard and Gail were striking out into new territory. Never before had they owned two pieces of property at once. The distance between the trailer parks and the apartment building was a little over a mile. They reasoned, however, that they could live in the apartment building and give someone in the trailer park free rent to merely oversee the premises and call them if any attention was needed. It was the thought of two pieces of property that was frightening. Between park and apartment building they would have double the number of mortgages, and they would have more than double the number of rentals, seventy-six units.

This last figure, on the other hand, also impressed them with its possibilities. (Remember, sales price increases $6 for each additional $1 per year of rent.) In twenty years the owner had put in only sparse maintenance. The apartment building, like their first one on Waverly, needed painting and improving. The trailer park was overgrown with weeds, and the roadway asphalt had deteriorated, leaving just dirt paths. Howard and Gail figured the trailer-park rentals of $40 a pad were low just as were the apartment building's $150 a unit (all units with two bedrooms). Hopefully, they could move in, improve both, and eventually raise rents, thereby giving them more immediate profit and more potential for profit on a future sale.

The price for both trailer park and apartment building was $323,-000, figured like this:

APARTMENT:

Sixteen units at $150 each	$ 28,800	(annually)
Less vacancy of 5%	1,440	
Less one unit as owner's or manager's apartment	1,800	
Total Income	$ 25,560	
	× 6	(cost factor)
	$153,360	

TRAILER PARK:

Sixty units at $40	$ 28,800	
Less vacancy factor of 0	0	
Less one unit as owner's or manager's apartment	480	
Total Income	$ 28,320	
	× 6	(cost factor)
	$169,920	
Total sales price for both properties	$323,000	(rounded)

There was one major obstacle. It turned out that the owner of the apartment building and trailer park, Mr. Thomas, did not want to trade. He said he was tired of living in an apartment building and tired of its headaches. He wanted his money out so that he could just put it in a bank and retire. Since he owned both properties free and clear, this would mean a tremendous tax burden for him even after he declared the whole amount as capital gains and paid taxes only on half. Howard pointed this out, but Mr. Thomas was adamant. He wanted his money in cash, and he was prepared to pay whatever taxes were necessary, regardless. (Believe me, there are more Mr. Thomases in the world than you might realize.)

Buying the property would normally be no problem, for Howard and Gail had an equity of $169,000 in Waverly Manor. Normally they would just sell for cash and buy Thomas's two properties. However, to avoid a heavy tax they had to trade. Even this would normally not be difficult. They would apply their $169,000 equity to Thomas's property and take out two loans for the balance of $153,000 to make up the total sales price of $323,000. (Howard and Gail wanted *two* loans as a safety precaution. Normally a lending institution gives a single loan on two pieces of property purchased in this way. But with two loans, if anything went wrong and the VanTills were forced into foreclosure, chances were that only *one* piece of property would be foreclosed and they could hold onto the other.)

However, Mr. Thomas would simply not trade, and as long as he insisted on not trading, they could not buy his properties. They had to have an exchange of equities in order to avoid losing a good part of their money in taxes.

Sometimes the best way through a problem is around it.

Howard came up with the solution. First he bought a six-month *option* from Mr. Thomas for $1,000 and then he and Gail put Waverly Manor up for sale. For readers unfamiliar with them, an option is an agreement that is open-ended for one party. It gives the buyer an opportunity to purchase a piece of property for a stated price and for stated terms *at some given time in the future*, in this case up to six months from the date of signing. For this privilege the buyer, Howard, paid $1,000 to the seller. If before the end of six months Howard bought the property, the $1,000 would be credited toward the purchase price. If he did not buy, he would lose his money. (Remember, Howard and Gail now have the additional income of the profits on the monthly rentals from Waverly Manor and raising $1,000 is not a big thing for them.)

For the $1,000, the seller of the option agrees to sell the property to the buyer according to the stated terms and at the stated price for the time period, in this case up to six months. He cannot sell to anyone else during the time period even if he gets a better offer.

Once he got his option on Mr. Thomas's property, Howard knew he and Gail had six months to make a deal. They immediately put Waverly Manor up for sale. What they wanted was a double escrow trade. All they had to find was a buyer for their apartment building to get it.

Mr. Breen was their man. Mr. Breen had just sold his bookbinding business and had made a sizeable profit on it. He wanted a single large investment such as an apartment building to gain a tax shelter. He was much in the same situation that the VanTills had been in when they first purchased Waverly Manor. Mr. Breen had roughly $200,000 from the sale of his business. He wanted to put most of that amount down and to secure a loan for the balance.

When Mr. Breen eventually made his cash offer, Howard and Gail invited him into their apartment and politely explained their position. They wanted a trade; otherwise a good portion of the money they received from Waverly Manor would be taxed. At first Mr. Breen was taken aback. He said they had not advertised a trade, only a straight-forward sale. Howard said that was true, but that here was what he and his wife had in mind: Mr. Breen wanted Waverly Manor. Howard and Gail wanted Mr. Thomas's property. Mr. Thomas wanted cash. If Mr. Breen would buy Mr. Thomas's property for cash, Howard and Gail would then trade with him (Figure 1).

FIGURE 1

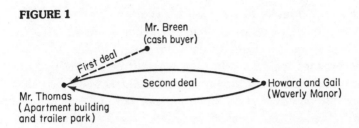

"Knowing you're right is only half; convincing others is the remaining half." COLUMBUS

Mr. Breen shook his head and looked puzzled. He was a simple bookbinder, he said, and this sounded all a bit complicated to him. Howard assured him that it sounded much more difficult than it really was. He said to think of it in terms of two separate deals. In the first deal Mr. Breen would buy Mr. Thomas's apartment building and trailer court. He would sign a deposit receipt with Mr. Thomas subject to certain conditions Howard said he would describe in just a moment. The deposit receipt would provide that Mr. Breen pay the agreed price of $323,000 for the property as follows: $169,000 cash and a note for the balance of $154,000 at no interest for *one day*. This would satisfy Mr. Thomas. This was escrow 1.

Now Mr. Thomas was out of the picture. He had sold his property and had gone off to retire (and pay taxes). There were just two parties left: Mr. Breen, who now owned a trailer court and apartment building he did not want, and the VanTills, who owned Waverly Manor. They would simply swap properties with no cash exchanged, giving Howard and Gail their desired tax-free exchange. This was escrow 2.

That was all well and good, Mr. Breen pointed out, but where was he going to get the $154,000 to pay off the one-day note for Mr. Thomas's property? He had only a total of $200,000 to spend. Now Gail stepped in and talked about those conditions in the deposit receipt Mr. Breen signed. The conditions were simply that Mr. Breen would pay off the $154,000 note with funds from escrow 2 and both escrows were to close (all deeds recorded and moneys paid out) at exactly the same time.

"Just a moment," Mr. Breen insisted, "how can escrow 2 close at the same time as escrow 1? I have to buy the first property before I can sell it, don't I?" Their discussion became animated at this point. "Yes," Gail answered, "but you need only own it for an instant, just a fraction. of a second, before you sell it. You will buy Mr. Thomas's two properties and trade them for ours in that order, but it will happen so fast that for all intents and purposes it will happen at the same time and both escrows will close simultaneously." As she went on to point out, double escrows are perfectly legal as long as *all parties concerned are completely aware of everything that is happening.* Before any documents were signed, Howard added, it would be necessary to get Mr. Thomas's assent to the deals.

"Assuming that everything works as you say," Mr. Breen asked, "where do *you* get the extra $154,000 to pay off Thomas?"

"That's easy," Howard explained, "but in order to understand it we have to jump ahead. Let's assume for just a moment that you have already bought Thomas's properties. You have $169,000 in equity and a one-day note for $154,000. Our equity (remember, Howard and Gail's equity is the sales price of $365,000 less the mortgages of $196,000) is roughly $169,000 also."

Sales price	$365,000
Less mortgages	196,000
VanTills' equity	$169,000

Howard continued. "Now we have the $169,000 to put down on Mr. Thomas's (your) properties. However, that is still $154,000 short of the asking price. To make up the difference, we get a new loan (actually two separate loans, one on Thomas's apartment building and another on his trailer park) for just that amount of money. Now we have the asking price."

Van Tills' equity	$169,000
Van Tills' new loans	154,000
Sales price of new property	$323,000

"While our equity is not in cash, our new loan is. We give you the $154,000 in cash."

"That's getting there," Mr. Breen said. "But what about my buying Waverly Manor? How does that work?"

"Simple," said Howard. "We merely trade our equities. You have $169,000 in equity in Thomas's properties, and that is exactly our equity in Waverly Manor. You can then either assume our current mortgages or add the $31,000 you have left from the $200,000 you originally wanted to invest and pay the mortgages down by that amount.

"As you can see, it works out quite well as a trade, *assuming that you have bought Mr. Thomas's properties first.* Because he is not willing to trade, this is the only way we can make the deal. I should point out that since both escrows close at the same time, all moneys and loans have to be in before the deal goes through—that means there is no risk that at any time you could lose any part of your money."

"It sounds okay to me," Mr. Breen said, "but you better put all those figures down on paper so I can reread them just to be sure I understand what you are saying. And I want to talk it over with my lawyer and accountant."

"The most important part of closing a deal is knowing when to stop talking." AN OLD REAL ESTATE BROKER

Howard wrote it all out for Mr. Breen. Then he presented the deals to Mr. Thomas, who gladly agreed to them; after all, he was getting all cash. One week later Mr. Breen called to say both his lawyer and accountant advised him to go ahead with the deal.

The only problem Howard and Gail ran into was with the escrow officers. It took them a long time to understand what was happening, but then Howard had once heard a Realtor say, "They're paid to be unimaginative."

The sale went off without a hitch. No cash passed through Howard and Gail's hands. They simply traded the equity they had in the property on Waverly Street as a down payment for the two properties Mr. Thomas had owned. They reported this as a tax-free trade on their income tax. (If an exchange is determined to have been made solely to avoid paying taxes, it may be disallowed. But that was not the case here.)

Howard and Gail immediately went to work repairing the two properties in the usual manner. They refurbished the new apartment house on Justin Street just as they had the building on Waverly. The trailer park, on Powell Street, took a bit more creative effort. They painted the clubhouse, of course. Then they repoured concrete on some pads which had partly disintegrated. Next they had all the roadways and many of the paths repaved with asphalt. Finally they added landscaping. They paid for these improvements out of the profits they had from their rental income. Within six months they had raised the rents from $150 to $175 on the sixteen apartments and from $40 to $50 on the trailer pads.

| Sixteen units rent raised $25 | monthly $400, annually $4,800 |
| Sixty units rent raised $10 | monthly $600, annually $7,200 |

Their gross rents now are:

APARTMENTS:		
Old rental rates	$28,800	
Increase	4,800	
Total	$33,600	
Less 5% vacancy factor	1,680	
Less one unit as owner's apartment	2,100	$29,820
TRAILER PARK:		
Old rent	$28,800	
Raise	7,200	
Total	$36,000	
No vacancy factor	0	
Less one unit as manager's apartment	600	$35,400
Total gross income		$65,220

If we multiply this by 6 we find that the VanTills' properties are now worth $391,320. Since their mortgage balance is roughly $154,-000, they have an equity of $237,320. More than a $60,000 increase in less than a year!

"Today an apartment building, tomorrow the world." HOWARD VANTILL

This brings us up to today on Howard's and Gail's progress in the Home and Income Reinvestment method. Their possibilities from this point on are almost infinite. They could make another tax-free trade for another apartment building or trailer park with low rentals and repeat their successful method. Or they could trade for a commercial building or even a vineyard. Or, if they so desired, they could sell for cash. Figuring capital gains, immediately half of their $237,-320 profit, or $118,660, would be theirs tax-free. They could then buy another apartment and shelter the remaining $118,660 from tax much in the same way they did when they sold the house on Justin Street. Note that each move they make defers the taxes they will have to pay. This is not to say they are escaping them, rather that they are just putting them off into the future. But since there is no ultimate time limit or limit on the number of such transactions that can be made (as long as no more than two or three are made in a single year), they can actually keep deferring their tax payment indefinitely. Meanwhile, if they choose, they can almost always take half the money (figuring capital gains) and spend it elsewhere.

But even if Howard and Gail *do nothing* with their equity, we must not forget their rental income. They are making a gross income of $65,000 (rounded) a year after taking into account vacancy factors and management on the two properties. Their taxes are roughly $21,000 a year. Their mortgage costs run approximately $15,600 annually. Assuming a reserve of $12,000 a year for maintenance and incidentals, or $1,000 a month, we come up with this result:

Gross income		$65,000
Taxes	$21,000	
Mortgage payments	15,600	
Reserve	12,000	
		48,600
Net income		$16,400

The VanTills are receiving back in cash roughly $16,400 a year. Because of depreciation on the properties virtually all this cash will be written off as a loss as was done on the Waverly Street property so that no tax will be paid on it. Nonetheless, it remains cash in their pockets to spend any way they want. It is $2,000 a year more than Howard's salary at the time. They can buy a new car, a boat, furs, another house. Or, if Howard should choose to, he could retire. And he and Gail do not have to worry about their equity. The rents will keep pace with inflation so that when it comes time to sell, their equity will have increased. This $16,400 a year is "pure gravy" for as long as they want it. Not bad for a $1,500 investment six years earlier!

You can't achieve success unless you really want it.

The Home and Income Property Reinvestment method is not guaranteed. It may not work for everyone. It assumes that the investor in the method has common sense, at least average luck, and the desire to succeed. If you lack one or more of these, stay away from it. If you have all these qualities, however, the method is the best possible plan for making large profits in real estate.

What are you waiting for? If you are going to buy a house anyhow (and more than three-fourths of us do), why not use this plan? All you have to lose is your poverty!

3

How to Buy Your First Home for Investment

LOCATION

This should be your single most important consideration. Always buy in the *best* neighborhood you can afford. This will give you the best opportunity for reselling. You can best find out what is a good neighborhood, assuming you are new to a community (even if you have lived there for a while you might get a big surprise) by contacting a half-dozen different Realtors. While they may all express slightly different opinions, they should give you a pretty good idea of which neighborhoods are economically sound and which are depressed.

DOWN PAYMENT

This is simply how much you can afford. I suggest you start small and work up. While the profits to be made on large investments are proportionally much larger than those on small investments, starting from the bottom gives you the experience you need to make the right decisions later on. Besides, it is always better to work with somebody else's money. I would say that in today's modern market about $1,500 is the minimum you should have (although it is, of course, possible to buy a house with no money invested at all—see Chapter 5 on solving the problem of financing).

LOAN: CREDIT RATING

The loan you will obtain on your first investment home will depend almost entirely on your credit rating and your ability to repay. In today's market there are more ways to finance a home than ever before. However, not everyone can qualify for every type of loan. Since credit is the key to financing, the various loans that are available have been arranged below in order of a borrower's credit standing. To find out approximately what you should be able to qualify for, first determine your highest credit rating, then check the loans listed there.

A Rating

You have excellent credit. You have charge accounts with at least two department stores, plus at least one bank credit card, plus oil company credit cards. In addition, you have no defaults, foreclosures, or repossessions on record. Presumably, in the last year you have taken out at least one loan from a bank or savings and loan institution, which you have repaid or are currently repaying. Further, you have been employed constantly for the last four years by the same company, or, if you have changed companies, you have always received a progressively higher salary. And finally, you must be able to earn at least 4½ times the monthly interest, principal, and tax payments *after* all your other monthly long-term debts have been paid. Only about 30 percent of the public qualifies for this category. You can qualify for all the following loans, and you can obtain a PMI (private mortgage-insured loan). This can be for *up to 95 percent of the selling price* of the house from virtually any savings and loan or mortgage banking institution. (See the section on private mortgage insured loans [PMIs] in Chapter 5 on financing for details.)

B Rating

Essentially the same as A only not quite as strong. You may not have borrowed and repaid a loan recently, may not have many credit cards, may not have worked at your present employment for more than a few years—in general you simply have not established your credit as strongly as an A. However, you must still be able to exceed your monthly payments of principal, taxes, and interest by four times with your gross income after all your monthly long-term debts have been paid. You can qualify for all the following loans plus an FHA loan or a GI loan (see details on government loans in Chapter 5), an FHA or VA (Veterans Administration) loan on a government-repossessed house (see section on government repossessions in Chapter 7 on foreclosures), an 80 to 90 percent loan from a savings and loan institution.

C Rating

You may have lost your car through repossession a few years ago, you may show some slow payments on credit-card purchases but you can explain these, and you may only make four times your monthly payment on interest, principal, and taxes, although you have been steadily employed at your present job for at least a year. You can qualify for all the following loans plus an FHA or VA loan on a government-repossessed home in a depressed area, an 80 percent savings and loan institution loan if you pay cash down to the loan (no seconds), a 75 percent bank loan if you obtain it from the bank where you regularly do business and have no bad credit experience with them, an 18 percent interest-plus loan from many of the finance and thrift companies (see Chapter 5 on financing), or a special government-assisted-housing-program loan.

D Rating

You have lost a house through foreclosure, but your car has been paid off promptly. You have a record of slow payments on credit-card purchases with an occasional repossession, although you also show many purchases where you have paid in time. You change jobs frequently or are making a salary less than four times your monthly payment in taxes, interest, and principal on the house you propose to buy. In general you have some bad credit as well as some good. You can qualify for all the following loans; also, the owner of the house you are trying to purchase may be persuaded to carry the loan, or you may be able to find private individuals with money to loan on property for interest rates 5 percent or more above normal who will be willing to advance you credit. You may be able to get a loan from the bank you do business with if you've borrowed and paid them back before.

F Rating

You have a long history of bad credit. You have never repaid a loan, never owned a car that was not repossessed, never owned a house that was not foreclosed upon, never made a payment on an item bought on a monthly-payment purchase plan. Such a credit rating is very difficult to establish because in the first place you must have gotten someone to loan you money before you could refuse to pay it back. Although I have met individuals with credit almost as bad as this, they are a rarity. Usually, bad credit or an F rating simply means a few marks against you and a lot of blank space on a credit form because you have not had time to establish a long credit history. You qualify for one of the best loans of all—an already established FHA or GI loan. This is a government loan that someone else has obtained on a piece of property and is willing to let you assume. (For problems involved see the discussion of government loans in Chapter 5 on financing.) In some depressed areas with high foreclosure rates, you can take over a house with as little as $100 or $200 down. (But I would think twice before I would sell my home to you!)

Note: These ratings are completely arbitrary and are used strictly to illustrate what persons of different levels of credit should be able to finance on today's market. Although many credit bureaus use a similar system, this rating scale was prepared only for this book.

HOW TO MAKE A PRO AND CON SHEET

This is simply a way for you as a buyer to organize your reasons for and against a particular purchase. While many people feel that they know their own minds, it has been my experience that one does not actually know how one feels until the feelings are put down on paper in black and white. I suggest the use of two kinds of pro and con sheets.

The first pro and con sheet should have to do with your attitude as a buyer. If you are planning to use the Home Reinvestment method, are you willing to make the sacrifices it demands? The best way to find out is to list all the demands which you feel are negative and also list all the positive rewards the program offers. Then you can make a sensible decision on whether or not you are ready to go ahead. A typical pro and con attitude sheet might look like this:

PRO:
1. The potential for making a lot of money
2. The possibility of eventual financial independence
3. Only a relatively short number of years spent in the plan
4. The opportunity to live in many different homes in probably much better neighborhoods than you could otherwise afford

CON:
1. The need to change homes often over an extended number of years

2. The need to choose a home for its investment value over and above your personal desires for what a home should offer
3. The requirement that you spend a lot of time and "elbow grease" fixing up property
4. The necessity of risking your money and future profits over and again on (real estate) deals
5. The trouble and effort involved in buying, selling, and renting homes and other real estate investments

If you can look at such a pro and con sheet and after reasonable consideration favor the pro side, you are ready to invest in real estate. If, on the other hand, being honest in your answers, you are not willing to make the required sacrifices, then you should stay out. The Home Reinvestment method is not for you.

Once you decide in favor of investing, all the following pro and con sheets will deal with specific pieces of property. You should never again need to weigh any of the considerations in the first pro and con attitude sheet. If you do, then you did not write it up honestly.

Many samples of pro and con sheets can be found in the preceding chapter, but these general rules are good to follow:

1. Be sure you list *all* the major disadvantages on the con sheet.

2. Do not forget to consider financing as either an advantage or a disadvantage on a particular home.

3. Do not forget to include the element of *time*. It may mean the difference between success or failure. If you have a loan due on a particular date and you cannot pay off, you may lose your entire investment.

WHEN TO MAKE AN OFFER

Although few people realize it, it takes a lot of courage to invest in real estate. You can look at dozens of houses, find the ideal investment opportunity for you, even conclude that there is no way to lose, but when it comes time to actually sign that check for the purchase of property, you may find your hand shaking a bit. This is particularly true with first investments. Once investors gain a bit of experience, they tend to move into new investments with a flair. But my experience is that there is always that twinge of remorse at the critical moment.

The only advice I can offer is that you be your own boss. Listen to others, but always make the final decision by yourself. No matter how much someone praises a piece of property or tells you not to purchase because you'll lose your money, decide for yourself when you are ready. That even applies to this book. I am simply recording facts as I have observed them. *There are no guarantees* that if you follow the plan outlined here you too will become successful. It may be your misfortune to lose at real estate. Every so often someone does. However, if you yourself have the courage to go ahead or not to go ahead, you will not have anyone but yourself to blame if things go wrong, and you will have no one but yourself to pat on the back if things go right. And further, you will gain the confidence to go on to bigger and grander projects.

There is the matter of precisely when to make an offer once you have decided on a piece of property. The best advice is to make it as soon as you possibly can once you have decided to go ahead. Once you have decided to buy, do not wait even an hour before you begin arranging to make an offer. There is always the chance that someone else may beat you to it.

If you are working through a Realtor, making an offer is a fairly simple procedure. Most brokers are well aware of the possibility of losing a deal because their offer came in just thirty minutes after the sellers signed an earlier one. They will work quickly too.

When purchasing a piece of property directly from the owner, I suggest this course. Both you and the owner go to an escrow or title insurance company or a lawyer (in states where members of the legal profession specialize in real estate sales) or even to a broker's office and there have a knowledgeable person draw up the appropriate sales forms. This is not to imply that sales forms are complicated. In general they are not. But by having them arranged by an independent third party you avoid any ill feelings either on your part or the seller's because of misunderstandings which might crop up before escrow closes and prevent the deal. In addition, there may be local laws one has to abide by in sales agreements which neither you nor the seller is aware of and which could conceivably negate the transaction.

In mentioning the possibility of going to a broker's office to draw up the forms, I am not speaking of paying a commission (if you and the seller are agreed, the broker is not really entitled to a commission). I am merely speaking of having the broker attend to the necessary forms for a set price, say $50 to $100. It will be money well spent.

TO WHOM TO MAKE OUT YOUR CHECK

The forms to sign are handled in detail in the next chapter, but every buyer should know this basic information.

In order to purchase a piece of property, it is necessary for the buyer to put up some money to indicate his willingness to go through with the deal. The amount can be anything over $1, but is usually from $500 to $1,000. It is commonly termed *earnest money*, which is descriptive of its purpose. The money you put up normally belongs to the seller and vouches for your intention to keep your part of the purchase agreement. Technically, if you fail to keep your end of the contract, that is, if you fail to follow through with the purchase, you will lose your earnest money. If the seller fails to follow through or the house is not marketable or there are other circumstances not your fault preventing the sale, your money will be returned.

The need for a deposit arises out of the time it takes to complete a real estate transaction. In contrast to the purchase of a piece of clothing or a car, a title search must normally be undertaken in the purchase of real property. This is done to ensure that the seller does in fact own what he is selling and hasn't encumbered it (added loans) other than those you were told about. In addition, the title search may reveal liens the seller was not even aware of that could affect his ability to transfer title to you.

The amount you put up as a deposit should be large enough to convince the seller you are sincere, yet small enough not to hurt you in the event you are unable to complete the transaction and lose it. Probably the safest way to protect your deposit comes from whom you make the payee of the check. While technically the money is the seller's, you do not have to write the check out to him. If you do and he cashes the check and the deal does not jell through no fault of your own, you may still not be able to get the deposit money back from the seller short of taking him to court.

I myself feel that the safest way to protect my deposit money is to make it a part of the sales agreement (deposit receipt) and make my check payable to an escrow officer. While the exact wording can vary greatly, I always include words to the effect that the check is the deposit on (address of property) and made part of the deposit receipt (date signed and seller's name). If I am working with a broker, he may insist on my making the check payable to him. If I feel that this is the only way to make the deal, I am sure to write the check out to the broker's *trust account*. This should make him as well as the seller responsible for the money. Seldom will the broker give the deposit money to the seller without the purchaser's written consent before the conclusion of the deal.

Since laws vary from state to state, I think it wise that before you make your first real estate investment you check with a local broker or lawyer and find out exactly what are the pertinent laws that affect you. This may cost you some money, but it will be well spent.

HOW LONG TO GIVE A SELLER TO SIGN

The number of days you give a broker to get a seller's signature is critical for psychological reasons. If a broker tells a seller he has a "hot buyer" who has to have an answer before midnight, the seller is forced to make a decision then and there on the merits of the offer. There is a kind of selling fever which occurs at such times and which usually impels a seller to sign. If, on the other hand, he has several days to make his decision, the fever may pass. He may decide to wait and see if perhaps a better offer will come in. He may not sign at all. Assuming the seller is local and can be easily reached, *I never give the broker more than one day to secure the seller's signature.*

CONTINGENCY CLAUSES

Many buyers insist on including *contingency clauses* in sales contracts. These are clauses that make the contract subject to some future event, such as the sale of the buyer's present home or the availability of low-interest financing. Almost invariably they contain the words "subject to." This weakens the contract and may provide an out *for the buyer* if he should decide to renege on the contract. Future financing may be poor, or he may not sell his present house—for any of countless different reasons, some possibly made up. If this happens, he can demand and be entitled to receive his deposit money back. When you are buying, the urge is great to include such a clause as it gives you greater protection and also delays the need for your having to conclusively decide in your own mind to buy. If you put such a clause in a sales agreement and the seller signs it, fine—you have really protected yourself. Unfortunately, what usually happens in such cases is that the seller refuses to sign because he fears justifiably that the contract is not binding. You may lose a good deal by using such contingency clauses.

HOW TO PSYCHOLOGICALLY
PREPARE YOURSELF

This is covered fairly extensively in Chapter 2 when Howard and Gail VanTill buy their first home, but I might add these few words. Unlike buying a pair of pants or a dress, buying a house involves a lot of "horse trading." While there may be an asking price, unlike the price of clothes it is subject to change.

Two forces are at play in a real estate transaction. The buyer is trying to get the lowest price he can; the seller is trying for the highest he can get. The final price usually depends on who is the best "horse trader." Unless you are unusually good and naturally talented at trading, here is what I consider sound advice.

As a buyer, decide on two prices. The best price you can reasonably hope to get the property for and the highest price you are willing to pay. When you make your offer, present the best, or lowest, price first.

Then become like a rock. Refuse to budge regardless of the pleas or threats of the broker or seller. A bit of acting helps here. You have to present a picture of tough-mindedness, of adamancy, even of "orneriness." But while refusing to move upward on your offer, you should listen carefully to the *tone* of the broker or seller. If he is working hard to convince you to come down; you are still in the bargaining stage. The fact that he is putting the pressure on indicates that he *still hopes a deal can be made.* Do not move from your ground at this stage. You may win.

When the broker or seller suddenly begins to lose interest, come out of your shell. This usually indicates that he has given up hope. He has decided that he has made the best counteroffer possible and that since it does not meet your original offer, no deal is possible. Now the seller will act. You know you have seen the lowest offer the seller will make. Now, you make a counter counteroffer. This can be the highest price you are willing to pay or something a bit lower, depending on what your judgment tells you the seller will do. If you counter, he may come back with another counter.

The danger is that you can begin enjoying this horse trading too much and not want to quit, even to the point of offering more than what you had earlier decided was the highest price you would go. Avoid the danger at all costs. If you give into it, likely as not you will buy a piece of property for more than it is worth to you. When you reach your highest price, *stop*. Refuse to budge *at all* from here on, even at the cost of losing the deal.

Here are two final points to keep in mind: (1) Often it is not price that you are haggling over, but terms, as was a case in Chapter 2. The same rules apply. (2) Experienced brokers or sellers know this game too. They are often not above a bit of acting themselves. Watch to see whether they are just *feigning disinterest* in order to get out your higher offer. For a beginner, a sure sign that you are being "taken" is for the broker or seller to jump immediately to write up your second offer. If he does this, you have been taken. Usually at this stage it takes a little convincing to get the other party to go along with you. After all, you have portrayed yourself thus far as a bit mean. Of course your seller or broker could even be feigning reluctance to take your offer when in reality he is dying to get you to sign. The only thing that helps here is experience.

WHEN TO INSIST ON POSSESSION

There is no set rule as to when is the best time to take possession of a piece of property, although usually it is given at the close of escrow. If the seller has some extenuating circumstances, such as a problem with the movers, it is not uncommon to give him a few extra days to move out. If, however, you have gained ownership and are paying taxes on a mortgage and the seller wants more than a few days, it is also customary to charge him rent. If you do not get possession at the close of escrow, the time the seller is to remain and the exact amount of rental for that time should be written out in special instructions and signed by the seller.

If you do not take possession at the close of escrow and the seller remains, you open yourself to the possibility of an event which, although rare, does occasionally happen: the seller who refuses to move. Perhaps he has become ill and cannot leave, or, more likely, financial causes such as a loss of employment make it expedient for him to remain. In such circumstances you may have to evict him through the same procedure you would use if he were a common tenant. (For further details see Chapter 2, when Howard and Gail VanTill evicted the Forgemans.)

Unless I am very familiar with the seller and know him to be hard hit by extenuating circumstances, I always insist on possession at the close of escrow. In fact, I include a provision in the escrow instructions for inspection of the premises either by me or by an independent person such as the broker to ensure that the seller has moved out. (Note: If you are selling and want thirty to sixty days to find a new home, your best bet may be to *delay the close of escrow* for this period of time.)

It is possible to take possession before escrow closes. This is normally done when the buyer needs a house to live in; then, rather than move into a rental and later move again into his new home, he rents his new home, by agreement with the seller, until close of escrow. The danger here is mostly to the seller. You as a buyer could move in as a tenant and then for some reason, such as your loan falling through, be unable to complete the deal. Now you have to move. If you do not, the seller's only recourse is to have you evicted as a common tenant

4

Don't Be Overwhelmed by Real Estate Forms

Have you ever taken your car in to a mechanic for repairs and had the following situation develop? You know that all the old buggy needs is to have the "thingamabobs" on the carburetor tuned up a little and it will run fine. But the mechanic says no, the venturis, the jets, and the needle and flow valves on the carburetor are all working perfectly. The car really needs an engine valve job and possibly a complete overhaul. (The price is $15 for adjusting the thingamabobs, but $100 to $350 for the other work.) You tell the mechanic you just know it can't be the valves; it's those things on the carburetor. He looks at you sternly and asks, "What things on the carburetor?" "You know," you reply, "those things that have to be twiddled with." He smiles condescendingly and says, "Who's the mechanic here, me or you?" In frustration you agree that he is and get the $100 plus job. The trouble, of course, is that chances are you were right, you just did not know the exact location of the items you were talking about, you did not know the terms to use, and you let yourself be bullied by the mechanic's overbearing attitude.

This same situation, unfortunately, can prevail in real estate deals. If you are the buyer or seller you may have a valid point to make, but because you are unfamiliar with real estate forms, you put the other party in a position of superiority. You can only *ask* how things can be done. You have to rely on the other person's good intentions to get them done your way. And if the other party (or broker) says you are wrong, your position becomes pathetic. You do not have the knowledge to *demand* and *insist*.

This chapter is designed to give you the basic insights into real estate forms so that when you are right, you will know it and be able to demand and insist and get away with it. It is designed to help you get the $15 thingamabob job instead of the $100 plus overhaul.

The first thing to understand is that real estate deals are almost always very simple. Even in the most sophisticated of transactions, the same basic forms and terms are nearly always used. If you list your house with a broker, you have a listing agreement. If you sell or buy property the document is usually a receipt of deposit. If you have a million-dollar apartment building, chances are you list it on the same listing agreement and sell with the same deposit receipt. These two forms are responsible for about 90 percent of all transactions. The other forms, which include deeds, escrow instructions, loan papers, employment verifications, termite reports, and title reports, are dependent on the first two. If the deposit receipt and listing agreement are drawn properly, then all the others should follow in due course, but since they are usually drawn up by escrow companies or lawyers who normally explain them carefully, they are not likely to become problem items, so we will deal with them later. First let us consider those two most important documents: the deposit receipt and the listing agreement.

DEPOSIT RECEIPT

A deposit receipt is ordinarily filled out by a broker (if one is involved in the deal) or by the seller. It is just what the words say it is: a receipt for the deposit the buyer is putting up on a piece of property. As mentioned, buying property is not like buying clothes or even a car. It is different because there is the necessity of *clearing title*, that is, determining that the seller does in fact own the property. If you decide to buy a $25,000 house, you do not just go to the seller and give him the money expecting he will write out a bill of sale. Before you give him your money, you want to be sure that he does in fact own the property he is selling and you want a bona fide *deed*—a document which conveys *title* (ownership) to you. This takes time. The normal procedure is for the buyer to put up *earnest money*.

Earnest money (as we've mentioned) is simply money that shows that a buyer is in earnest about buying the property. It vouches for his intentions—if the buyer changes his mind and refuses to go through with the sale before title is transferred, the earnest money is forfeited and goes to the seller. The seller is enticed into going through the procedure of giving clear title because he knows that either his property will be sold or he will receive the deposit. Usually, the more money, the more earnest the buyer.

The seller (or the broker who acts as the seller's agent) writes out a *receipt for deposit*, which is normally in the form of a personal check. A sample deposit receipt is shown in Figure 2.

I always include all the following items on all deposit receipts I sign:

1. The full names of all parties
2. A legal or acceptable description of the property
3. How the buyer will take title (joint tenants, single person, etc.)
4. How the deposit is to be applied; the terms of the loans
5. The time for the sale to conclude
6. The date and signatures of all parties

The deposit receipt binds the deal. It specifies exactly what will happen to the money the buyer puts up. It also usually specifies that·if certain conditions are not met—for example, if the seller is not able to convey clear title—the buyer is to receive his deposit back.

The items just mentioned are for the protection of all parties—they

FIGURE 2*

CALIFORNIA REAL ESTATE ASSOCIATION STANDARD FORM

REAL ESTATE PURCHASE CONTRACT AND RECEIPT FOR DEPOSIT

THIS IS MORE THAN A RECEIPT FOR MONEY. IT MAY BE A LEGALLY BINDING CONTRACT. READ IT CAREFULLY.

_____, California, _____, 19____

Received from_____ herein called Buyer,

the sum of _____ Dollars ($_____)

evidenced by cash ☐, personal check ☐, cashier's check ☐, or_____as deposit on account of

purchase price of_____ Dollars, ($ _____)

for the purchase of property, situated in_____, County of _____,

California, described as follows: _____

_____

1. Buyer will deposit in escrow with_____the balance of purchase price as follows:

_____
_____
_____
_____
_____
_____
_____
_____
_____

Set forth above any terms and conditions of a factual nature applicable to this sale, such as financing, prior sale of other property, the matter of structural pest control inspection, repairs and personal property to be included in the sale.

2. Title is to be free of liens, encumbrances, easements, restrictions, rights and conditions of record or known to Seller, other than the following: _____

Seller shall furnish to Buyer at _____ expense a standard California Land Title Association policy issued by _____ Company, showing title vested in Buyer subject only to liens, encumbrances, easements, restrictions, rights and conditions of record as set forth above. If Seller fails to deliver title as herein provided, Buyer at his option may terminate this agreement and any deposit shall thereupon be returned to him.

3. Property taxes, premiums on insurance acceptable to Buyer, rents, interest, and_____ [insert in blank any other items of income or expense to be prorated] shall be prorated as of (1) the date of recordation of deed or (2)_____

[Strike (1) if (2) is used]. The amount of any bond or assessment which is a lien shall be paid / assumed [Strike one] by Seller. Seller shall pay cost of documentary stamps on deed.

4. Possession shall be delivered to Buyer [Strike inapplicable alternatives] (a) on close of escrow, or (b) not later than _____ days after closing escrow, or (c)_____

5. Escrow instructions signed by Buyer and Seller shall be delivered to the escrow holder within _____ days from the Seller's acceptance hereof and shall provide for closing within _____ days from the Seller's acceptance hereof, subject to written extensions signed by Buyer and Seller.

6. Unless otherwise designated in the escrow instructions of Buyer, title shall vest as follows: _____

[The manner of taking title may have significant legal and tax consequences. Therefore, give this matter serious consideration.]

7. If the improvements on the property are destroyed or materially damaged prior to close of escrow, then, on demand by Buyer, any deposit made by Buyer shall be returned to him and this contract thereupon shall terminate.

8. If Buyer fails to complete said purchase as herein provided by reason of any default of Buyer, Seller shall be released from his obligation to sell the property to Buyer and may proceed against Buyer upon any claim or remedy which he may have in law or equity; provided, however, that by placing their initials here, Buyer: ( ) Seller: ( ). Buyer and Seller agree that it would be impractical or extremely difficult to fix actual damages in case of Buyer's default, that the amount of the deposit is a reasonable estimate of the damages, and that Seller shall retain the deposit as his sole right to damages.

9. Buyer's signature hereon constitutes an offer to Seller to purchase the real estate described above. Unless acceptance hereof is signed by Seller and the signed copy delivered to Buyer, either in person or by mail to the address shown below, within _____ days hereof, this offer shall be deemed revoked and the deposit shall be returned to Buyer.

10. Time is of the essence of this contract.

Real Estate Broker _____ By_____

Address_____ Telephone_____

The undersigned Buyer offers and agrees to buy the above described property on the terms and conditions above stated and acknowledges receipt of a copy hereof.

Address_____ Buyer_____

Telephone_____ Buyer_____

ACCEPTANCE

The undersigned Seller accepts the foregoing offer and agrees to sell the property described thereon on the terms and conditions therein set forth.

The undersigned Seller has employed_____ as Broker(s) and for the Broker(s) services agrees to pay Broker(s) as a commission, the sum of_____Dollars ($_____) payable as follows: (a) On recordation of the deed or other evidence of title, or (b) if completion of sale is prevented by default of Seller, upon Seller's default, or (c) if completion of sale is prevented by default of Buyer, only if and when Seller collects the damages from Buyer, by suit or otherwise, and then in an amount not to exceed one half that portion of the damages collected after first deducting title and escrow expenses and the expenses of collection, if any.

The undersigned acknowledges receipt of a copy hereof and authorizes Broker(s) to deliver a signed copy of it to Buyer.

Dated:_____Address_____ Seller_____

Telephone_____ Seller_____

Broker(s) consent to the foregoing. Broker_____ Broker_____

Dated:_____ By_____ Dated:_____ By_____

A REAL ESTATE BROKER IS THE PERSON QUALIFIED TO ADVISE ON REAL ESTATE. IF YOU DESIRE LEGAL ADVICE CONSULT YOUR ATTORNEY. THIS STANDARDIZED DOCUMENT FOR USE IN SIMPLE TRANSACTIONS HAS BEEN APPROVED BY THE CALIFORNIA REAL ESTATE ASSOCIATION AND THE STATE BAR OF CALIFORNIA IN FORM ONLY. NO REPRESENTATION IS MADE AS TO THE LEGAL VALIDITY OF ANY PROVISION OR THE ADEQUACY OF ANY PROVISION IN ANY SPECIFIC TRANSACTION. IT SHOULD NOT BE USED IN COMPLEX TRANSACTIONS OR WITH EXTENSIVE RIDERS OR ADDITIONS.

Copyright 1971 by California Real Estate Association   FORM NO. D-14   (Rev. 6-71)

*Courtesy of the California Real Estate Association.

strive to avoid misunderstandings that could sour a deal. If any of these items were not in a deposit receipt prepared for me, I would refuse to sign until they were included or a very good explanation of why they were not in there was given (which is not too likely). If the broker or seller refused to include them but insisted that the deal was all right and I was still in doubt, I would refuse to sign until I had consulted a lawyer or an independent other broker. I have found an excellent rule of business that should be etched on every check and note is that in most cases, *your signature does not protect you—it protects the person you are giving it to*. Generally speaking, once you have signed and money has passed hands, you are committed. If you are troubled by any aspect of a document, resolve the problem before you sign. It may cost you money if you wait till later.

One other caution is in order. While it is not *usually* necessary for all the wording to be in precise language since the deposit receipt by its very nature tends to be an informal document, the wording should not be elusive; that is, it should not be vague. If you are going to get a loan for 9 percent, the agreement should state 9 percent, not "high-interest loan." If there is going to be a second trust deed, the deposit receipt should say second trust deed and include the exact amount, length of time to be repaid, rate of interest, and monthly payment; and if the monthly payment does not pay it all back, the deposit receipt should state that there will be a balloon payment and indicate when during the length of the loan it will occur. It should not say something like "seller to give buyer a second loan for remaining balance of purchase price."

LISTING AGREEMENT

You will only come in contact with a listing agreement if you are *selling your property through a broker*. It is the document that empowers the broker to find a buyer for you and to take a deposit from the buyer for you (the seller). You can be sure the broker will have a listing agreement ready for you to sign, for without it he might not be able to collect his commission. Remember, the broker in most

FIGURE 3*

EXCLUSIVE AUTHORIZATION AND RIGHT TO SELL
CALIFORNIA REAL ESTATE ASSOCIATION STANDARD FORM

1. **Right to Sell.** I hereby employ and grant _____,
hereinafter called "Agent", the exclusive and irrevocable right to sell or exchange the real property situated in
_____, County of _____, California described as follows:

_____
_____
_____
_____

2. **Term.** Agent's right to sell shall commence on _____, 19____ and expire at midnight on
_____, 19____.

3. **Terms of Sale.**
(a) The price for the property shall be the sum of $_____, to be paid as follows:

_____

(b) The following items of personal property are to be included in the above-stated price:

_____

(c) Agent is hereby authorized to accept on my behalf a deposit upon the purchase price in an amount to
be not less than $_____.

(d) Evidence of title to the property shall be in the form of a California Land Title Association Standard
Coverage Policy of Title Insurance in the amount of the selling price to be paid for by _____.

(e) I warrant that I am the owner of the property or have the authority to execute this agreement. I
hereby agree to permit a FOR SALE sign to be placed on my property by Agent named herein.

4. **Compensation to Agent.** I hereby agree to compensate Agent as follows:

(a) _____% of the selling price if the property is sold during the term hereof, or any extension thereof, by
Agent, on the terms herein set forth or any other price and terms I may accept, or through any other person,
or by me, or _____% of the price shown in 3(a), if said property is withdrawn from sale, transferred, conveyed,
leased without the consent of Agent, or made unmarketable by my voluntary act during the term hereof or any
extension thereof.

(b) the compensation provided for in subparagraph (a) above if property is sold, conveyed or otherwise
transferred within 90 days after the termination of this authority or any extension thereof to anyone with whom
Agent has had negotiations prior to final termination, provided I have received notice in writing, including the
names of the prospective purchasers, before or upon termination of this agreement or any extension thereof.
However, I shall not be obligated to pay the compensation provided for in subparagraph (a) if a valid listing
agreement is entered into during the term of said 90 days protection period with another licensed real estate
broker and a sale, lease or exchange of the property is made during the term of said 90 days protection period.

5. If action be instituted on this agreement to collect compensation or commissions, I agree to pay such sum
as the Court may fix as reasonable attorney's fees.

6. I authorize the Agent named herein to cooperate with sub-agents.

7. This property is offered without respect to race, creed, color, or national origin.

8. In the event of an exchange, permission is hereby given Agent to represent all parties and collect compensation or commissions from them, provided there is full disclosure to all principals of such agency. Agent is
authorized to divide with other agents such compensation or commissions in any manner acceptable to them.

9. I agree to hold Agent harmless from any liability or damages arising from any incorrect information sup-
plied by me or any information I fail to supply.

10. Other provisions: _____

_____

11. I acknowledge that I have read and understand this Agreement, and that I have received a copy hereof.

Dated _____, 19____ _____, California

_____	_____
Owner	Owner
_____	_____
Address	City - State - Phone

12. In consideration of the execution of the foregoing, the undersigned Agent agrees to be diligent in endeav-
oring to obtain a purchaser.

_____	_____
Agent	Address - City
By _____	
	Phone	Date

For these forms address California Real Estate Association
505 Shatto Place, Los Angeles 90020. All rights reserved.   **FORM A-11**
Copyright 1972 by California Real Estate Association

*Courtesy of the California Real Estate Association.

instances works for the *seller;* he is the seller's agent. (Realtors are committed by their code of ethics to watch out for the interests of all parties.) It is possible for the broker to work only as an agent for the buyer in attempts to find a piece of property, but this is rare. Figure 3 shows a typical listing agreement.

Like the deposit receipt, the listing agreement is usually a made-up form with spaces left blank which the broker fills in. I always check to see the listing agreement includes the following:

1. The property address
2. The date
3. The name of the broker
4. The sales price
5. The terms I am willing to accept
6. The down payment I want
7. The percent of the sale I will pay in commission
8. *The amount of time the listing is in effect*
9. The broker's and my (seller's) signatures

The listing agreement does not normally commit you to sell your property. It does commit you to pay a commission to the broker you name as your agent if and when he brings in a buyer who is *ready, willing, and able* to buy. It is conceivable, although it rarely happens, that a seller will sign a listing agreement for ninety days and after one month decide that he does not want to sell for personal reasons. If the broker in the meantime should have found a buyer ready, willing, and able to purchase, theoretically the broker could sue the seller for his full commission claiming that he had fulfilled his part of the bargain. (Agency laws can differ from state to state, and if in doubt, you can check with several brokers before signing an agreement.)

An important item in a listing agreement is that it specify the exact length of time the agency is in force. (An agency is similar to the arrangement that show-business people have with someone who gets them show dates. The agent is simply one who is authorized to represent another person.) If there is no termination date, conceivably the listing could be in force until the house is sold. This could be a great disadvantage if (1) you as the seller decided not to sell at a later date, or (2) it turned out that the broker did not work very hard at selling your property and you wanted to change brokers. Be sure there is a definite termination date.

Another important item is the commission. Sometimes sellers do not realize that in virtually all areas the commission amount is set at the time the listing is signed—rarely is there a law which specifies the amount. Since commissions are usually paid in terms of a percent of a sales price, you can sign up with a broker at anywhere from 1 to 99 percent. On residential property 5 to 6 percent is fairly common.

I can still vividly remember an argument I had with a real estate agent several years ago who wanted to list a house I owned and was renting out. I was satisfied that her firm would do a good job and I did not have time to find a buyer myself, so I was ready to sign the listing agreement. When checking it over, however, I noticed that she had inserted a 7 percent listing commission and had given a termination date six months hence. When I called these to her attention she curtly informed me that *all* listing agreements were for six months and 7 percent—*it was the law*.

I insisted there was no such law. The agreement was whatever we decided, and the most I would give was 5 percent and three months. The house was well priced, and with reasonable effort she should be able to sell within that length of time. The going rate for commissions in the area was then 5 percent.

The agent balked. She said that I was trying to cheat her out of her rightful money, that I was trying to break the law, that if I wanted her to spend her time and money on my property, then I would have to give her enough time and a high enough rate of commission to make it worthwhile—in short, I was a cheapskate.

When I pointed out that 5 percent was the normal rate of commission and that if she could not find a buyer in three months she was not worth having as an agent in any event, she began behaving in a manner I have rarely seen salespeople behave in. On one hand she threatened to take me before the real estate board (I was acting here as simply a seller and not a broker) and on the other said she would compromise at five months and 6 percent.

At this point I showed her to the door. I told her that if this was the way she behaved in front of me, I could expect that as my agent she would act the same way before potential buyers. If she misrepresented the truth to me, she would do the same to them. If she tried to coerce me into signing a listing, she would very likely try to coerce a buyer into signing a deposit receipt. In short, if I was not satisfied with her handling of me, I could be fairly sure that I would not be satisfied with her handling of my buyers. And further, if she acted this way now, how would she act when she found a buyer, got an earnest-money deposit, and brought in a deposit receipt for a deal that might not be to my liking? Would she again try to force me to sign something I did not want to sign? I told her that her manner convinced me that I would never sign an agreement with her or the firm she represented, and further, that I was sending a letter to her broker describing her actions and sending copies to both the local real estate board and the state real estate commissioner. Needless to say, she was contrite when she left. There are times when showing someone the door out is the best conclusion of a deal.

Another point with regard to listings is that normally the listing agreement will specify that the agent is allowed to take a deposit (earnest money) for you, the seller, for the price and terms you specify. However, rarely will the agent be able to find a buyer who offers exactly what you are asking. The buyer may want to pay less or may want you, the seller, to take back a second loan, or any of a dozen other things may be different from what is on the listing agreement. If the agent brings in a deposit receipt for anything other than what your listing agreement specified, he is bringing in an *offer*. This means that you have the option of accepting or rejecting it *without paying a commission*. The only time you are obligated to pay a commission without signing a deposit receipt is when the offer is for exactly the terms of the listing. Even then you probably are not committed to sell, only to pay a commission.

There are several types of listings that you can give an agent (note: Agent and broker are used synonymously):

Exclusive-Agency Listing

This usually gives one broker the right to sell your property for a specified time. Under this agreement, no other brokers can sell it. It does not however, prevent you from selling "by owner" and not paying a commission.

Exclusive-Right-to-Sell Listing

This normally gives the broker the sole right to sell. You have to pay a commission even if you sell the property yourself.

Open Listing

In most states this gives more than one broker the right to sell your property. You can list with two or twenty. If you sell it yourself, there is no commission to pay.

Verbal Listing

This is simply your verbal consent to list. If you are very honest and your word is your bond, the broker can collect his commission if he comes in with a buyer. But if you do not want to pay, there is almost no way he can collect. In some areas this type of listing is not considered legal. Unless a broker knows you very well, he will not normally work on a verbal listing.

Multiple Listing

In areas that have real estate boards, this is a convenient listing that many brokers use. Usually it is an exclusive-right-to-sell Listing (you have to pay a commission even if you sell it by yourself) that contains a clause allowing the broker to share the listing with all the other members of his real estate board. They agree on commission splits within the group, and you effectively list your house with dozens or even hundreds of brokers by signing with just one. This differs with the open listing in two ways. First, as just mentioned, you have to pay a commission even if you sell yourself; second, the agreement you have is with *all* the members of the real estate board and with all for exactly the same terms. (A real estate board is simply a group of brokers banded together and dedicated to helping each other and, by doing so, the selling public.)

Net Listing

This can be any of the previously mentioned listings, except that the commission, instead of being a percentage of the sales price, is simply whatever the broker can get over and above what you want. The "net" amount is what you, the seller, specify as the money you are to receive if a sale is made. Say, for example, it is $25,000. The broker's commission is anything over that amount he can get. If the house sells for $26,000 (forgetting other costs for a moment), the broker gets $1,000. If, however, it sells for $35,000, his commission is $10,000. This type of commission is often used with land or other highly speculative properties.

Which listing is best? When I am selling a house, I always give the *exclusive-right-to-sell listing*. I do not mind if the broker wants to include the multiple listing as long as I am confident he will work hard on the deal himself. I have seen too many cases where a broker takes a listing, "puts it on the multiple service," and forgets about it. If another broker gets a buyer, good for the seller. But the original broker, feeling just getting the listing is the job, does no more work.

There are what are called *listing offices* and *selling offices*. The brokers in the former are interested only in listing property and putting it on the multiple service. They rarely find buyers and make sales themselves. They let brokers from selling offices find the buyers. Here the brokers are looking for buyers for homes listed by other brokers on the multiple-listing service. They rarely take the time to find their own listings. When I want to list I will always choose a selling office. Here I know the broker will work to sell my property. When I want to buy I check out all the listing offices. There is always a chance they have something they did not put on the multiple that the selling office cannot show me.

How to tell them apart? A selling office generally advertises more, has more salespeople, and has the appearance of great activity. It, after all, has many deals under way all the time. A listing office is usually a broker alone or with one or two salespeople. The pace of the office is slow, and the salespeople may actually seem awkward handling a buyer; after all, they have few. But do not belittle such offices. They often have a very good word-of-mouth reputation, and their friends and friends of friends, etc., go there to list. Good deals can be found in quiet offices.

THE OFFER

As a principal (a buyer or seller, but not a broker), I have found the following to be the best way of handling an offer, particularly when I am unfamiliar with any aspect of the deal. When I am selling and the broker brings the offer in, I have him explain it thoroughly, and I ask questions on any part I am uncertain about. When he has completed his presentation, I thank him and tell him I will need some time (at least a few hours) to consider. Under no circumstances do I sign while he is there unless the offer is for exactly what I was asking. Often a broker will protest. He is afraid that I, the seller, will look at the deal closely and find some reason not to sign; perhaps I will think it over and decide that the price is too low. Or I may not like the terms being offered, or any of a dozen other variables may disturb me. The broker will assert pressure to get me to sign. Remember, he gets no commission until a deal is made. He does not want to take the chance of my finding some reason not to. But I always refuse, insisting that I need time to think it over by myself. And I always get the time. There is virtually no deal that cannot wait a few hours. If there is some technical part of the deposit-receipt contract that I do not understand, I take it to a lawyer or another broker. It is amazing how an independent third party can remove one's doubts, or confirm them. And if the deal is sound, the broker need not have worried: I will sign it. If it is not and a third party shows me why, it is much better for me that I did not sign. In this case I usually return the offer to the broker and give him the opportunity of correcting the deficiency.

THE COUNTEROFFER

As mentioned, the deposit receipt is the contract for the sale of real estate. However, it is not binding unless *both buyer and seller have signed*. Simply for a buyer to have put up earnest money and signed a deposit receipt does not mean that he has bought the property. The seller has to sign the same agreement before a sale is made. If a broker brings me (the seller) an offer that contains deficiencies, such as a lower price, less down payment, or other poorer terms than I agreed to in the listing, I may make a counteroffer.

A counteroffer usually works in this manner. Either on the same piece of paper that the buyer's deposit receipt is drawn up on or on a new form, I have the broker write out the exact terms I want. These could be the original terms in the listing agreement, or I could modify them somewhat. A buyer offers $23,000 on the deposit receipt. I counteroffer at $24,000. A new deposit receipt is drawn up with the buyer's name included. Then I sign it and ask the broker to present it. If now the buyer signs, we have a deal. If not, he may counter-counteroffer at, for example, $23,500. There is no deal until both buyer and seller *agree on exactly the same terms*.

I once haggled to three o'clock in the morning over a sale until finally there was just $150 separating me, the seller, and the buyer. At this point it became evident that neither I nor the buyer would budge another dollar. In this case, to make the deal, the broker put in the

$150 from his commission. (I would not count on this happening every time, but it does occur.)

The broker is the person under the gun. As mentioned earlier, the broker is normally the agent for the seller, although those brokers who are members of the National Association of Realtors are committed to watching out for the interests of both buyer and seller. As I have noted, these are called Realtors. The broker is the person who because of circumstance is the most interested in making the deal. After all, in nearly all cases, he or she gets paid nothing unless a sale is made.

In my experience, having dealt with brokers and having been one in the past for a long number of years, I have found that almost always they will go out of their way to protect the interests of *both* the buyer and the seller. They know that a large part of their business, whether it be in single-family residential or multimillion-dollar commercial buildings comes from repeated dealings and from personal recommendations by satisfied customers. Brokers who expect to last, and most real estate salespeople do have this goal, know they have to build up good reputations. Probably the best way to find a scrupulously honest real estate broker is to find one who has *actively* been in business (actually sold, not just held on to a license) for fifteen to twenty years. Just having lasted that long is testimonial to the good job that broker does.

5

How to Successfully Borrow Money on Real Estate

If you have ever gone to a bank to get a loan, you have undoubtedly realized one thing: if you do not really need it, they will give it to you, but if you're down and out, broke, and really need the money, there is not a chance in the world you will get the loan. While this may seem inhumane and is sometimes cruel, it underlies the basic way all loans work today—they are a business venture in which a lender puts up a certain amount of cash in hopes of getting a certain return in the form of interest. Making a loan is rather like going into business, and the only goal is profit.

Until forty or fifty years ago what was needed to get a loan was good character and a handshake, but those days are gone. Lenders will not put their money in trust today, particularly in real estate. They want a *guarantee* that one way or another they will at least get every cent they invest back. They are willing to risk the potential interest, but never any capital. This underlies a basic law of borrowing: *You can never borrow more than you already have.*

The way this operates is by the use of *collateral*. This is another word for security and means simply that if you want to borrow $10, you have to put up something worth $10 to secure the debt, such as a watch or a tennis racket. If you want to borrow $100,000, you have to put up something worth that amount, like an apartment building or expensive house. No collateral, no loan. Of course, putting up real estate does not mean giving up the use of it. You are still entitled to enjoy the property as long as you maintain the payments on the loan. Technically this is called *hypothecation*.

Let us assume for a moment that a home buyer wants to obtain a loan to make a purchase. The first question that arises in the mind of the lender is how much is the home the buyer wants (his collateral) worth? All real estate loans (technically called trust deeds or mortgages, but for our purposes the word "loan" will suffice) are based on an *appraised value*.

Appraised value for the purpose of financing is the total amount the property will bring in a sale as estimated by the person loaning the money. Large lending institutions such as banks, savings and loan companies, and insurance companies hire trained personnel who do nothing but appraise property for them. Individuals who personally loan money, on the other hand, usually will make the appraisal themselves.

The two most common methods of appraising residential property are the *comparison method* and the *replacement method*. The comparison method involves finding houses that have sold recently and that are similar, or as close to identical as possible, to the house being appraised. A comparison of the sales figures will indicate the going market value for the property. This is similar to the method used to appraise the value of used cars. If you have a 1974 Chevrolet and want to know what it is worth, find out what other 1974 Chevrolets with the same equipment as yours are selling for and you will have your answer. Of course, the comparison method has one built-in defect—in actual practice, no two houses are identical, and in all but tract areas it may be very difficult to find any two houses that are even very much alike. In cases such as this, the replacement method of appraisal is used.

In the replacement method, the value of the land is separated from the value of the house. Next, the value of the land is determined by the comparison method. (Normally, land is land, although allowances are made for different lot sizes, views, hills, etc.) Now the value of the house is determined by figuring what it would cost to completely replace it if it were to be built today. This is done by use of a cost-per-square-foot figure. Any local builder can tell you what the square-foot cost in his area is at any time. Because of inflation, it is constantly rising. In the early fifties it took about $10 a square foot to build a typical home. In the early seventies it took well over $20, and every indication is that it will take well over $40 in a few years.

For an example, let us assume the builders in a locality are figuring $20 a square foot to build a house. The appraiser now determines how many square feet are in the house in question. (This is done from the outside with a tape measure. Simply find the width of the house, then the length, and multiply the two figures to get the square footage. For odd-shaped houses, divide the house into boxes or squares, multiply each area separately, then add all figures together. Garages are normally included if they are enclosed and attached.) If the house has 2,000 square feet and the cost is $20 a square foot to build, it would cost $40,000 to replace the house. Add the $40,000 to the price of the land and you have the appraised value by the replacement method.

Appraisals can vary by as much as 10 percent, depending on how the appraiser "feels" about the property. Condition, landscaping, carpeting and drapes, and quality of neighborhood all enter this realm of intangibles.

An appraisal, then, is basically a statement of opinion, and it is possible to influence the person making the appraisal. For example, often an owner preparing to sell is not sure how much to ask. He may request that a lending institution send out their appraiser to give him an estimate of how much they will loan to a buyer when he gets one.

There is usually no charge for this service. However, once the appraiser gets to the house, he may tend to be a bit conservative. Although the lender is in business to make loans, he wants only to make safe ones, and if he can make them for a little bit under the *market value* (which simply means the amount a house should sell for given a reasonable amount of time and a reasonable amount of exposure to potential buyers), he can protect himself in the event of foreclosure. The appraiser knows this, and he may appraise a house at $24,000 rather than the $25,000 it may actually be worth.

On the other hand, if a seller calls for an appraiser and says that he has the house up for sale at $26,000 and has had "several nibbles" at that price the appraiser may extend his appraisal that high in order to make the loan pending a sale for that amount.

One common error that sellers make when trying to influence appraisers' decisions is to try to oversell them on the property. I have gone to make appraisals and have been met by anxious sellers who plied me with coffee and cake, who pointed out the nice furnishings, the smart choice of colors, and the extensive landscaping. While taking all these into account, I was much more interested in such things as the number of square feet in the house, any cracks that could indicate structural damage, and the general appearance of the neighborhood. Too much attention may make an appraiser suspicious that the seller has something to hide.

It is best to let an appraiser see the property undisturbed but to confront him with solid facts and figures. If you can show him that the price you are asking is reasonable for the house and the area, two out of three times he will go along with you.

It is important to understand at this point that the appraised value of a piece of property is not the amount that a lender will loan. Each type of lender will loan only a percentage of appraised value called the *loan value*. Banks, for example, will usually only loan up to 90 percent of the appraised value. Under certain conditions federal savings and loans will lend up to 95 percent of appraised value.

Here is an example to show what "up to" means. Suppose the

appraised value of a house is $30,000. A federal savings and loan institution under certain conditions (which we will go into shortly) will loan 95 percent of this appraisal, or $28,500. This means that a financially strong potential buyer need only produce a $1,500 down payment to make the purchase. However, if the buyer is not strong, the lender may be willing to loan only 90 percent, or $27,000, meaning the buyer has to come up with $3,000. If the buyer is very weak, the lending institution may not be willing to loan anything at all.

You, as a buyer of real estate, normally want to obtain the highest possible leverage (the smallest down payment and the highest loan) so that the smallest amount of your money will be tied up. The reason for this is quite simple. If you have $3,000 to invest and you have to put it all down, as in the 90 percent loan above, you can buy only one house. But if you need put only $1,500 down, you have the potential of buying at least two houses. (The difference in monthly payments between a 90 percent and a 95 percent loan is usually negligible.)

This matter of the strength or weakness of a borrower brings us to a second law of borrowing, and it is that *you have to demonstrate that you can pay back what you borrow with interest*. A trustworthy smile and a handshake are not sufficient here either. There are basically two ways you demonstrate your ability to repay with interest. The first is by showing that your income from your regular employment (if you are buying a house) or from the property itself (in the case of apartment and commercial buildings) is large enough to pay back the monthly installments on the loan. Assuming you are the prospective borrower buying a house, you commonly have to make in regular income anywhere from 4 to 4½ times the monthly payment just to qualify for the basic loan. The way the monthly payment is determined is not mysterious. Three factors are taken into account:

1. The monthly payment on the loan's *principal* and *interest*
2. One-twelfth of the year's taxes
3. One-twelfth of the year's fire insurance

Here is a typical example on a $30,000 house:

1. Principal and interest $200 a month (for thirty years) $200
2. $800 taxes divided by 12, or $67.   67
3. $96 insurance divided by 12, or $8   8
                                     Monthly payment $275

This monthly payment is now multiplied in a minimum buyer by 4 to give the minimum income necessary to qualify for the loan on a $30,000 house:

$$\begin{array}{r} \$\ 275 \\ \times 4 \\ \hline \$1,100 \end{array}$$

The minimum amount you need to make a month to qualify for the loan is $1,100.

It should be explained here how monthly salary is arrived at. If you have a weekly wage, you take the amount before taxes and other deductions and multiply it by 4.3 (the average number of weeks in a month). If you get paid every other week, you multiply it by 2.15.

As we have said, in this case the *minimum* a borrower has to make is four times the monthly payment to qualify for the loan. However, at four times he might just get a minimum loan, say 80 percent of the appraised value. On the other hand, if he made more money and qualified at, say, 4½ times the monthly payment, he might get a 90 percent loan. If his income were 4½ times the monthly income, he might even get a loan for 95 percent of the appraised value, or he might not get a loan at all—because of the second way (besides income) a borrower demonstrates his ability to pay back what he borrows with interest, his "track record." As the type of property changes from a house to an apartment or commercial building, this factor becomes all-important.

TRACK RECORD

The "track record" is simply a buyer's past performance at borrowing money. The term, naturally enough, derives from the racetrack, where it refers to the number of wins and losses of a given horse. The more winning performances and the fewer losing ones, the better the track record and the more likely someone will bet on the horse. The same holds true for a potential borrower. The more loans he has successfully paid back in the past, the more likely it is that someone will loan money to him again. It should be pointed out, however, that in racing simply not having any losses at the track is not a good track record by itself. Consider the case of the racehorse that has never run before. It has no track record at all; hence very few will bet on it. A borrower with no established credit is much in the same situation.

How to Establish a Good Track Record

There is much that can be done to improve your chances of getting a good loan. Let us assume you are purchasing your first home. If you have no track record at all but have a good job, it is a good idea to establish a track record at least a year before you go to buy. Take out one or two credit cards and use them occasionally, and go to a bank and borrow a small sum of money. Once you have a few credit cards, this should be no problem. Put the money you borrow from the bank back into it (it can be the same one) to draw the highest interest and then pay it back—a loan of six months is usually sufficient. Except for the running around, you can accomplish this at a small cost, since the difference between the interest you owe on the loan and the amount you receive from your deposit should be no more than 4 percent (if you borrow $500 for *six months* at 12 percent and receive 5 percent on it when it is deposited, it costs you only $17.50 for the money). Now when you go to buy you will have a minimum track record but an impressive one. Nothing impresses a lender more than to see that a potential borrower has taken out a bank loan and repaid it.

Now let us turn to the more common case of an individual who has a long track record, some of it good and some of it bad. Perhaps you suspect, or a broker has told you, that your track record is too poor to allow you to get a loan. Assuming that your gross pay is enough to qualify you for your loan, here are several things you can do to make a bad record look better.

First, consider your job. Even if you make enough to qualify, lenders are sticklers for length of time on the job. If you have not worked at your current job for at least three years, you are suspect. They fear that you may be laid off. The way to get around this is to list all the jobs you have had during at least the past three years, emphasizing that each time you changed you received a higher rate of pay. If there is no room for this on the regular loan application, write it down on a separate sheet of paper and insist on its being attached.

If it is not possible to make this statement truthfully, then make a similar list and for each time you accepted lower pay give a good solid reason why, such as better fringe benefits, shorter hours, improved working conditions, or a workplace closer to home. If you can show that you remained in the same occupation, this will help also. Remember, loan applications are read by people and not machines. If there is a reasonable explanation, it may be accepted.

Second, consider your *credit report*. This is probably the single most important document in your loan application. It is crucial that you obtain a copy so that you can see where you are given bad marks and so that you can challenge them. For some unknown reason, credit companies will rarely release to borrowers copies of the reports they send lenders. Some relief can be obtained through the Fair Credit Reporting Act of 1971. This law really affects only credit bureaus which transmit and collect information on bill paying and which conduct interviews with former employers and neighbors. In many cases the law requires the credit reporting company to disclose much of the information in its files to the borrower (medical and certain other information may be withheld). Getting it, however, may be another matter. If the credit company refuses to disclose its file or if the borrower thinks he is not seeing the entire report, his recourse is to appeal to the Federal Trade Commission—a process which can be time-consuming and which may in the end still not yield the desired information. If you are working through a broker, a much simpler way may present itself. The broker often will be able to simply supply you with a copy of your report. If not, a good way to get one is to have a friend, preferably one who has stationery with a business letterhead on it, order it. It will cost you $10 or $15, but it will be well worth it.

Once you get a copy of the credit report on yourself, examine it closely. It is nice to consider all the favorable aspects, but do not dwell on them. Consider the unfavorable parts and prepare a challenge. In order to do this, it is necessary to have at least a working knowledge of how credit reporting agencies operate. (For more detailed discussion of credit ratings see again Chapter 3.)

When a borrower applies for a real estate loan, most lending institutions require a credit report. In every city there are established credit companies. (Retail Credit is the country's largest and probably used most often.)

Credit companies usually have two main sources of information. The first is the many department stores and credit-card companies which report slow payments and repossessions. These are usually listed in chronological order in the report. The second source is personal contact. Many times the credit company will send out a representative who will talk to your *neighbors* about your character. Occasionally, the representative may talk to you, the borrower. Although much of this information is basically hearsay, it often ends up in the report and can be the most damaging part of it. Once this procedure is done, it is usually not repeated for a substantial period of time.

After you have a copy of the credit report on yourself, check the notices of slow payment or repossessions. Occasionally there will be some that are in error. Usually, however, these notices reflect the borrower's habits over as long as the previous ten years. Challenging all bad marks whether true or not is a common practice in improving one's credit report. But never challenge the credit company on this score; remember, it is merely repeating what someone else has said. Instead, you must now go to the original source.

If a department store says it repossessed a piece of furniture from you and you are sure you never bought anything there, write the department store and if necessary go there in person. Such things usually can be straightened out, and once the store's mistake is cleared up, request the store to send an explanation to the credit company and a copy to you.

If, on the other hand, a piece of furniture was repossessed, your only option is to write the department store and ask for its clemency. You can explain extenuating circumstances. Once the store responds to you, offering it a sum of money as partial payment for a loss it suffered may change its whole attitude regarding you. If you can demonstrate that, for example, you could not pay then because you were out of work but have since found employment and are now willing to pay back at least some of the money owed, the store may even reextend you its own credit. (The store has undoubtedly written off the loss you caused it on its taxes.) And it may be willing to write that all-important letter. If you have five bad marks against you, you may be able to improve three of them this way.

Now check the report's comments, if any, on your character. If they are bad, your best option is probably to try for a second report. To do this, have your friend request another report insisting that a personal check be made. This can usually be done for a fraction of the cost of the first report. Now go around to your neighbors and inform them that someone from a credit agency will be coming by and request that they give the best possible report on your character. Unless you are really a bad character, they will usually comply.

You will find out how successful you have been when you receive the report from your friend. Typically it will note the bad marks given on the first report but will also note that in a follow-up good marks were given. You can also now check to see if the earlier bad marks from any department store that sent a letter requesting their removal were made. If they were not, now is the time to send a copy of the letter from the store to the credit company and demand that the changes be made. (Still keep at least one copy for yourself to show the lender if all else fails.)

But what if you have nothing but a bad track record? If all you have is bad marks, I suggest you forget about credit reports altogether. Concentrate on getting loans that require no credit evaluation, as is the case with the assumption of some existing government loans, to be explained shortly.

This leads us to the final aspect of the track record—how well the borrower has done buying and selling real estate. This matter is particularly acute when you are purchasing income property. Before a lender will loan you 75 percent on a $400,000 apartment building, or $300,000, he wants to see that you have successfully handled other real estate transactions and, hopefully, that you have some apartment management experience. If you have a first-rate track record in this field, he probably will not care what your personal credit report has to say.

Improving Your Track Record on Real Estate Deals

This is quite easy, usually. The important thing to remember here is that if you have suffered a foreclosure on a piece of property, this fact rarely appears in any credit report. Unlike credit-card companies and department stores, lenders rarely report to credit agencies. About the only place knowledge of a foreclosure appears is in public records, usually only of the county in which it occurred, and in the local newspaper, where it is printed for a few days. Credit agencies often try to pick up such information and add it to their files, but the volume of foreclosures is so great and the cross referencing required would be so expensive to maintain, that most of the information rarely gets in. If a lender is particularly suspicious, he can hire a credit agency to go back many years checking old records; however, the cost here is usually prohibitive.

Therefore, to build up your track record on real estate deals, you need only list all the properties you have owned and successfully sold. This is extremely effective in presenting a blue-ribbon track record, particularly if any foreclosures you may have had were in another county.

A word of caution needs to be added here. Some loan-application forms require that you list *all* the property you have owned over a period of time. Failure to list a piece of real estate here may result in loss of the loan. Also, some borrowers have a period of bad luck and lose a lot of property through foreclosure. They often get a reputation which spreads among lenders. Nothing in the world can improve a bad track record that is dispersed by word of mouth.

We have just covered the way real estate loans operate—now on to the specific types of loans available today.

FHA LOANS

The government, through the Federal Housing Administration, started promoting the sale of residential property during the early 1930s, the dark days of the last depression. Because of economic conditions then it was extremely difficult for the average person to come up with the one-half to one-third usually required for a down payment. The FHA changed all that by making it possible for a person to purchase a home with as little as 3 percent down. In no small way the government's actions through the FHA were responsible for the enormous housing industry we have today.

How the FHA Works

The Federal Housing Administration normally does not loan money itself (although exceptions to this occur in poverty and rural areas and in the case of low-income families who could not normally qualify for other loans). Rather than loan money itself, the FHA *insures* the money of lenders. It is like a gigantic insurance company. When a borrower gets an FHA loan, he or she gets it from a bank or other lending institution. The function of the FHA is to guarantee that in the event the borrower defaults, the loan will be paid back to the lending institution. Note: An FHA loan does not guarantee the person who borrows the money. It guarantees the money of the institution that loans it.

The Cost of an FHA Loan

For the guarantee of a loan, the FHA charges the *borrower* ½ of 1 percent per year on the unpaid balance. The lender collects this amount with the regular monthly payments and forwards it to the government. Unlike other governmental agencies, the FHA is completely self-sustaining in this, its primary function. It has to make up any losses on loans it has guaranteed out of its own funds, the ½ of 1 percent paid on every loan. It is a tribute to the fine concept of this organization that during its over four decades of service it not only has paid back to the general funds of the government all the money that was used to start it, but has always maintained reserves large enough to handle all defaults. It in effect has always shown a profit.

The Advantage of an FHA Loan

The great advantage FHA loans have over all conventional (nongovernment) loans is that when it is time to sell, the new buyer can *assume* the old loan at the old rate of interest. This is particularly crucial during times of high inflation when interest rates are also high. Owners of homes with old, large FHA loans on them usually have no trouble at all selling. Buyers flock to their door, for they can sell at an interest rate of 5, 6, or 7 percent, whereas new loans are going from 7 to 11 percent. Even newer FHA loans are substantially lower than conventional interest rates. (Recheck Gail and Howard VanTill's first sale in Chapter 2.)

New FHA Loans

To take the *buyer's* side on a new loan, he normally prefers an FHA loan for three reasons: first, the interest rate is fixed by the government and is usually lower than for conventional loans. Second, by law he can only pay 1 point. (A point is normally considered the equivalent of $\frac{1}{4}$ of 1 percent of the difference between the FHA interest and the going rate for conventional loans.) It is a one-time fee paid when the loan is first obtained. If the FHA interest rate is $8\frac{1}{2}$ percent and conventional loans are going for 10 percent, the usual fee could be 6 points. On a $10,000 loan this is $600. The buyer only pays $100, or 1 point, however. And third, since the FHA inspects houses thoroughly before clearing loans and usually requires the seller to correct any deficiencies such as termite damage or a bad roof or water heater, the buyer can be fairly sure that with an FHA loan he is getting a house in good condition.

Disadvantages of an FHA Loan

FHA loans have come into considerable disfavor in recent years, and their percentage of the total real estate mortgages issued has declined since 1969. The major reason for this is, ironically, what was just spoken of as an advantage to the buyer—the points. In our previous example the difference between the going rate for an FHA and a conventional loan was $1\frac{1}{2}$ percent, which we translated into 6 points. (Note: This equation—1 point = $\frac{1}{4}$ percent—is an approximation. In actual cases the availability of money and confidence in the economy also play a big part. I have seen the requirements as high as 15 points when the difference in interest rates was only $2\frac{1}{2}$ percent.)

As stated, the buyer by law can only pay 1 point. In the above case of a $10,000 loan, that is $100, and the seller is left to pay the remaining 5 points, or $500. Since this fee is added on above already-stiff closing costs and, in many cases, broker's costs, most sellers, naturally enough, are reluctant to sell to a buyer who wants to obtain a new FHA loan. Remember, we are talking now of getting a *new*

FHA loan. (In the section on advantages we talked of a seller disposing of his property which had an *existing* FHA loan on it—a very different matter.)

In addition, the appraisals of the property can take anywhere from two weeks to three months to obtain, and to get FHA approval of the buyer can take an equally long period of time. These delays also put a damper on new FHA sales.

Why Are Points Charged?

Points do not go to the FHA. They go to the person or institution making the loan. They are a sort of bonus for giving money at lower than normal interest rates. It has been argued that lenders' rates on FHAs are lower than on conventional loans because, after all, they are government-guaranteed. Unfortunately, most lenders feel that, guarantee or not, they want the highest rate of interest available on their money. Adding points is one way of getting it.

How to Get a New FHA Loan

You as an individual cannot arrange an FHA loan yourself. To get one, you must go to a bank or savings and loan institution or to a mortgage banker. Since the decision on making such a loan is not up to the lender, but to the FHA, it does not matter which type of institution you choose. The only thing to remember is that the amount of points varies from lender to lender. It might pay off to shop around, particularly if you are the seller.

Most people who have bought or sold real estate through a broker are aware that the broker usually arranges the loan. This is a convenience he provides buyer and seller and is part of the service for which he charges a commission. (There are almost never kickbacks or fees paid to brokers by lenders for getting FHA loans.) There is no reason at all, however, why you as a buyer or seller cannot go to a lender direct. In actual fact many do, and often. Simply approach the loan officer in your bank or other lending institution and explain what you want. He will be more than happy to handle all the details and paper work.

Qualifying the Buyer for a New FHA Loan As mentioned earlier, in order to get any loan, the buyer must be able to pay back the loan with interest. Here is what is required of a buyer who wants to get an FHA loan, as described in an FHA bulletin which was recently issued by a lender. Keep in mind, however, that regulations are constantly changing. A check with any lender can bring you up to date.

INCOME: Generally speaking, the buyer's monthly income should equal $4\frac{1}{2}$ times his monthly housing expense. If the buyer is making installment payments on a car, furniture, or something else having six or more months to run, then the total of these payments is deducted from his gross income to determine his effective income. Overtime, part-time-employment income, and child-support payments received are generally not considered effective income in qualifying a buyer for a long-term mortgage. Any income that cannot be expected to continue for at least one-third of the term of the loan will not be considered.

CREDIT: Tardiness in making payments should be explained in full by the buyer—the reason for the slow payments and what attempts have been made to work out satisfactory arrangements. Bankruptcy is in itself not a reason for rejection. However, if sufficient time has not elapsed since the bankruptcy for the buyer to have reestablished his credit references, approval would be doubtful.

Qualifying the House FHA appraisals by a certified appraiser are issued for six months on existing construction, one year on proposed construction, and may be extended for one additional six-month or one-year period. The property will be reinspected at the time of extensions. The fees vary but are in the $50 range.

INTENT: The buyer must intend to occupy the property (or one unit if it is larger than a single-family dwelling) himself. He cannot be purchasing it exclusively to rent out.

FHA appraisal amounts are frequently predicated on certain repairs being made. These are listed by attachment to the appraisal. When the repairs are completed, the mortgagee requests the FHA to inspect the required work and issue its acceptance that the repairs have been completed to the FHA's satisfaction. Repairs not done or done in a haphazard manner can be rejected, causing loss or delay of the loan.

FHA Technical Data

Tables 5-1 and 5-2, which follow, represent an effort to make the

Table 5-1
FHA SECTION 203B
Owner-Occupant, Existing Dwelling, 1 to 4 Units

MAXIMUM LOAN
$45,000   1 unit
48,750   2–3 units
56,000   4 units

DOWN PAYMENT
Based on sales price plus closing costs, or FHA value including closing costs, WHICHEVER IS LESS. FHA loans are made in increments of $50, rounded down.
3% of first $25,000
10% of next $10,000
20% of balance

NONOCCUPANT MORTGAGES
85% of maximum loan as computed above.

IF THE BUYER IS A VETERAN (FHA-VA)
(served on active duty not less than 90 days, discharged other than dishonorably)
0% of first $25,000
10% of next $10,000
15% of the balance

VETERAN TERMS ARE AVAILABLE ON SINGLE UNITS ONLY.

VETERAN TERMS ARE AVAILABLE EVEN IF BUYER HAS PREVIOUSLY OBTAINED A VA LOAN.

TERM OF LOAN
30 years or three-fourths of remaining economic life of property, whichever is less.

Table 5-2

Income Conversions

Per hour	Per week	Per month	Per year	Per hour	Per week	Per month	Per year
1.65	66.00	286.00	3,432.00	4.00	160.00	693.33	8,320.00
1.70	68.00	294.67	3,536.00	4.05	162.00	702.00	8,424.00
1.75	70.00	303.33	3,640.00	4.10	164.00	710.67	8,528.00
1.80	72.00	312.00	3,744.00	4.15	166.00	719.33	8,632.00
1.85	74.00	320.67	3,848.00	4.20	168.00	728.00	8,736.00
1.90	76.00	329.33	3,952.00	4.25	170.00	736.67	8,840.00
1.95	78.00	338.00	4,056.00	4.30	172.00	745.33	8,944.00
2.00	80.00	346.67	4,160.00	4.35	174.00	754.00	9,048.00
2.05	82.00	355.33	4,264.00	4.40	176.00	762.67	9,152.00
2.10	84.00	364.00	4,368.00	4.45	178.00	771.31	9,256.00
2.15	86.00	372.67	4,472.00	4.50	180.00	780.00	9,360.00
2.20	88.00	381.33	4,576.00	4.55	182.00	788.67	9,464.00
2.25	90.00	390.00	4,680.00	4.60	184.00	797.33	9,568.00
2.30	92.00	398.67	4,784.00	4.65	186.00	806.00	9,672.00
2.35	94.00	407.33	4,888.00	4.70	188.00	814.67	9,776.00
2.40	96.00	416.00	4,992.00	4.75	190.00	823.33	9,880.00
2.45	98.00	424.67	5,096.00	4.80	192.00	832.00	9,984.00
2.50	100.00	433.33	5,200.00	4.85	194.00	840.67	10,088.00
2.55	102.00	442.00	5,304.00	4.90	196.00	849.33	10,192.00
2.60	104.00	450.67	5,408.00	4.95	198.00	858.00	10,296.00
2.65	106.00	459.33	5,512.00	5.00	200.00	866.66	10,400.00

Income to Monthly-Payment Ratios

Monthly payment including taxes, ins.	Income required at:		
	4 to 1	4½ to 1	5 to 1
90	360.00	405.00	450.00
91	364.00	410.00	455.00
92	368.00	414.00	460.00
93	372.00	419.00	465.00
94	376.00	423.00	470.00
95	380.00	428.00	475.00
96	384.00	432.00	480.00
97	388.00	436.00	485.00
98	392.00	441.00	490.00
99	396.00	445.00	495.00
100	400.00	450.00	500.00
101	404.00	454.00	505.00
102	408.00	459.00	510.00
103	412.00	463.00	515.00
104	416.00	468.00	520.00
105	420.00	472.00	525.00
106	424.00	477.00	530.00
107	428.00	481.00	535.00
108	432.00	486.00	540.00
109	436.00	490.00	545.00
110	440.00	495.00	550.00
115	460.00	518.00	575.00
120	480.00	540.00	600.00
125	500.00	563.00	625.00
130	520.00	585.00	650.00
135	540.00	608.00	675.00
140	560.00	630.00	700.00
145	580.00	653.00	725.00

2.70	108.00	468.00	5,616.00
2.75	110.00	476.67	5,720.00
2.80	112.00	485.33	5,824.00
2.85	114.00	494.00	5,928.00
2.90	116.00	502.67	6,032.00
2.95	118.00	511.33	6,136.00
3.00	120.00	520.00	6,240.00
3.05	122.00	528.67	6,344.00
3.10	124.00	537.33	6,448.00
3.15	126.00	546.00	6,552.00
3.20	128.00	554.67	6,656.00
3.25	130.00	563.33	6,760.00
3.30	132.00	572.00	6,864.00
3.35	134.00	580.67	6,968.00
3.40	136.00	589.33	7,072.00
3.45	138.00	598.00	7,176.00
3.50	140.00	606.67	7,280.00
3.55	142.00	615.33	7,384.00
3.60	144.00	624.00	7,488.00
3.65	146.00	632.67	7,592.00
3.70	148.00	641.33	7,696.00
3.75	150.00	650.00	7,800.00
3.80	152.00	658.67	7,904.00
3.85	154.00	667.33	8,008.00
3.90	156.00	676.00	8,112.00
3.95	158.00	684.67	8,216.00

5.05	202.00	875.27	10,504.00
5.10	204.00	884.00	10,608.00
5.20	208.00	901.34	10,816.00
5.30	212.00	918.67	11,024.00
5.40	216.00	936.00	11,232.00
5.50	220.00	953.34	11,440.00
5.60	224.00	970.67	11,648.00
5.70	228.00	988.00	11,856.00
5.80	232.00	1005.34	12,064.00
5.90	236.00	1022.67	12,272.00
6.00	240.00	1040.00	12,480.00
6.10	244.00	1057.33	12,688.00
6.20	248.00	1074.67	12,896.00
6.30	252.00	1092.00	13,104.00
6.40	256.00	1109.33	13,312.00
6.50	260.00	1126.67	13,520.00
6.60	264.00	1144.00	13,728.00
6.70	268.00	1161.33	13,936.00
6.80	272.00	1178.67	14,144.00
6.90	276.00	1196.00	14,352.00
7.00	280.00	1213.33	14,560.00
7.10	284.00	1230.67	14,768.00
7.20	288.00	1248.00	14,976.00
7.30	292.00	1265.33	15,184.00
7.40	296.00	1282.67	15,392.00
7.50	300.00	1300.00	15,600.00

150	600.00	675.00	750.00
155	620.00	698.00	775.00
160	640.00	720.00	800.00
165	660.00	743.00	825.00
170	680.00	765.00	850.00
175	700.00	788.00	875.00
180	720.00	810.00	900.00
185	740.00	833.00	925.00
190	760.00	855.00	950.00
200	800.00	900.00	1000.00
205	820.00	923.00	1025.00
210	840.00	945.00	1050.00
215	860.00	968.00	1075.00
220	880.00	990.00	1100.00
225	900.00	1013.00	1125.00
230	920.00	1035.00	1150.00
235	940.00	1058.00	1175.00
240	960.00	1080.00	1200.00
245	980.00	1103.00	1225.00
250	1000.00	1125.00	1250.00
255	1020.00	1148.00	1275.00
260	1040.00	1170.00	1300.00
265	1060.00	1193.00	1325.00
270	1080.00	1215.00	1350.00
275	1100.00	1238.00	1375.00
280	1120.00	1260.00	1400.00
285	1140.00	1283.00	1425.00
290	1160.00	1305.00	1450.00
295	1180.00	1328.00	1475.00
300	1200.00	1350.00	1500.00
310	1240.00	1395.00	1550.00
320	1280.00	1440.00	1600.00
330	1320.00	1485.00	1650.00
340	1360.00	1530.00	1700.00
350	1400.00	1575.00	1750.00

clearest and most complete possible presentation of the most commonly used new loans that are available through FHA. It must be remembered, however, that the government is constantly changing and updating the program, so that these tables should be used primarily as a guide. At the time you decide to get a new FHA loan, check with the lender for any possible changes that may have occurred.

FHA Closing Costs

These costs vary slightly from state to state depending on the type of loan, whether mortgage or trust deed. Here is a typical example:

BUYER'S COSTS:
1. Down payment (must be buyer's own money—cannot be borrowed)
2. One point (maximum)
3. One-half of escrow fee—not to exceed $65 (except in Arizona)
4. Recording deeds
5. Tax service contract
6. Credit report
7. ALTA (American Land Title Association) (lender's title policy)
8. Appraisal fee
9. *Impounds*—one month mortgage insurance, two months fire insurance, tax impounds (minimum)
10. Tax proration
11. Adjusted interest on new loan

SELLER'S COSTS:
1. Points
2. Escrow fee—all over $65 (except in Arizona)
3. Revenue stamps

4. Owner's title policy
5. Payoff of existing liens
6. Proration of taxes, etc.
7. Termite clearance and FHA-required repairs
8. Broker's commission

Items 2 through 8 of the buyer's costs may be paid by seller under any FHA program; however, this may affect the loan amount, since it is based on the buyer's total cost. Items 9 through 11 must be paid in cash by the buyer.

VA LOANS

The government's veteran's loan program is designed to help veterans obtain decent housing at low down payments. You must be a veteran or on active duty with the armed services to qualify for a *new* VA (also called GI) loan. Once the loan is on the house, like the similar FHA loans, anyone can assume it. (However, the VA tends to be more rigid in supervising the assumption of its loans.) One of the best available ways to buy is to take over an existing VA loan—it gives the buyer low interest rates and the ability to resell later with the advantage that someone else can take over the loan.

How Do They Work?

The Veterans Administration Guaranteed Loan program was started in 1944 as the Serviceman's Readjustment Act. It provides a guarantee to the lender (just like the FHA loan is guaranteed) of an amount not to exceed $17,500. What this means is that if a loan is given for $25,000 and the buyer defaults, the VA will pay the lender $17,500. This leaves a balance of $7,500 unpaid. However, since most houses are worth at least this amount in a foreclosure sale, the lender is usually more than willing to make the loan

Interest Rates and Points

Like FHA loans, the VA sets a limit on the interest that can be charged. Since this is often below the amount conventional loans are getting, lenders charge points to make up the difference. In times of high interest rates, points can be very high. I have seen points as high as 22 during one week late in 1973.

Here are the technical data on VA loans. Once again, the reader is urged to check with the VA for updating and changes.

Who Can Qualify?

The buyer must be one of the following three:

1. He must have been on active duty during World War II or the Korean conflict and (*a*) discharged or released other than dishonorably having served ninety days or more, any part of which was during the period from September 16, 1944, to July 24, 1947, or from June 27, 1950, to January 31, 1955, or (*b*) discharged by reason of service-connected disability from periods of active duty, any part of which occurred during either of the above two wartime periods.

2. He must have been on active duty after January 31, 1955, discharged or released other than dishonorably, and have been on continuous active duty for 181 days or more, any part of which occurred after January 13, 1955, or have been discharged from active duty by reason of a service-connected disability.

3. He must be presently on active duty (other than for training purposes) and have served at least 181 days in that status.

(Note: Veterans with World War I service only are not eligible. The Congress is continually setting expiration dates for VA benefits and continually extending them. It is a good idea to call a lender to be sure the program you qualify for has not by chance expired, before you make a deposit on a house.)

Qualifying the Property

Like the FHA, the VA appraises the property; however, unlike the FHA it issues a certificate of reasonable value, or CRV. This states the *maximum* price the veteran can pay for the property and still get the loan. This is done to protect the veteran from paying an exorbitant price for his home.

Down Payment

There is no down payment, providing the price does not exceed the CRV. On VA loans there is also no maximum loan. It is left up to an agreement between the borrower and the lender, although the amount the VA guarantees never goes higher than $17,500. As you can see, on a $30,000 house this is more than half the price and a good guarantee, but on a $70,000 house it is only a fourth of the price. To a lender the guarantee decreases in worth as the price of the property increases. Loans are generally written for thirty years.

Reinstating a VA Loan

Should the veteran sell the house and the buyer *not* assume the loan, but rather pay it off, either obtaining a different loan or paying cash, the veteran may reinstate his loan by applying to the VA. This means that potentially a veteran can use his eligibility over and over again.

Originally VA loans only guaranteed the first $4,000 to a lender. This was changed to $7,500 in 1950 and to the current $17,500 in 1975. This can mean a bonus to veterans of World War II and Korea, even if they used up all their original eligibility. The veteran who obtained his loan prior to May 7, 1968, may have $10,000 remaining (the difference between the $7,500 he used and the current allowance of $17,500). The veteran who obtained his loan prior to April 20, 1950, may have as much as $13,500 remaining

VA and FHA Default Penalty

When a veteran uses his eligibility to get a VA loan, he promises to repay the money to the government. If he defaults and the VA has to pay the lender the guaranteed amount up to $17,500, the VA then can turn around and sue the veteran for the money. In actual practice this rarely happens, for when a person loses his house, he is normally so deep in insolvency that suing him will do no good. There is an important exception, however. If you as a veteran purchase your house and obtain a VA loan and then at some later date turn around and sell the property, allowing the new buyer to assume the loan, your liability to the VA normally *does not end*. Many unsuspecting veterans have been caught in this snare. Should the second buyer default on the house, the VA may then come back and sue the veteran who was the original owner for the loss. Since it is very likely that this vet will be solvent, the suit could cost him a good deal of money, up to $17,500 plus costs. The same principle applies to FHA loans.

Closing Costs on a VA Loan

For the buyer:

1. No down payment normally required
2. One percent origination fee (maximum)
3. No escrow fee
4. Recording deed of trust
5. Tax service contract
6. Credit report
7. ALTA (lender's title insurance policy)
8. Fire insurance and tax impounds (two-month minimum)
9. Tax proration
10. Adjusted interest on new loan
11. Appraisal fee (only if veteran's name is on the CRV)

The seller *may* pay any or all of the veteran's costs. The seller's costs are essentially the same as for an FHA loan.

Table 5-3 is an estimate of typical buyer's closing costs on either an FHA or a VA loan.

Table 5-3

Estimate of buyer's closing costs for either FHA or VA insured loans:

Sales price or value	Buyer's closing costs*
$ 8,000–11,000	$250
11,000–14,000	300
14,000–18,000	350
18,000–23,000	400
23,000–28,000	450
28,000–34,000	500
34,000–40,000	550

*Will vary on the time of year purchased according to the amount of taxes and insurance required for impounds.

No Penalties on Government Loans

Unlike conventional loans, there is no prepayment penalty on either FHA or GI (VA) loans. A prepayment penalty is a sum of money, usually six months interest or 2 percent of the loan, that the lender charges if the loan is paid off before the date it is due.

CONVENTIONAL LOANS

A conventional loan is simply any mortgage or trust deed that is not a government-insured loan. There are six major sources of this type of financing, and we shall consider each in detail.

Banks

Commercial banks are among the most conservative of lenders when it comes to real estate, and also among the best. They will, for example, make personal loans, whereas almost no other lending institution will. The great problem is that banks will not loan a very high percentage of the appraised value of a piece of property. Usually about 90 percent is the most, and 75 percent is not uncommon. While this may seem a very low percentage when compared with the low down payments available through the government programs, it is well to remember that banks make their primary conventional loans on large apartment and commercial buildings which government loans cannot be used for. (Banks also fund GI and FHA loans, but that is not our concern here.) When you want to buy a trailer park or vineyard or apartment house, go to a bank for the financing and be prepared to put at least 20 percent down. But when you want to buy a house and want to put the minimum down, do not go to a bank (except to secure a government loan). Loans on real estate are only one part, and a relatively small part at that (usually 25 percent), of the bank's total business; therefore it is usually not willing to go out on a limb to make a property loan.

In general, the following is true about bank loans: banks almost never make second, or subsidiary, loans; they are only concerned in primary financing, or first loans. Banks' interest rates on real estate are indirectly related to the prime rate, which is the rate they charge their very best customers, which are giant corporations. The loans they make on real estate are often *1 percent less* than the prime rate. The reason for this is twofold: first, the collateral on real estate, the property, is easily repossessed, hence very secure; and second, there is a ready secondary mortgage market—a system where the banks can sell the loan in order to get new money to make more loans. Banks will make short-term personal loans. The going rate for these is usually 4 to 8 percent above the prime rate, depending on the borrower's track record

If you are just starting out and you go to borrow $1,000 on a personal note to use as a down payment on a piece of property, you may find stiff opposition. You will be required to fill out extensive credit reports and verifications of employment and salary which your employer must sign, and you will have to give a detailed description of why you want to borrow the money. It is very likely that you will be turned down, for banks in general do not like to loan money to someone to use as a down payment where another loan is involved. However, as your track record improves and your *net worth* gets higher (net worth is simply the total amount you owe subtracted from the total amount you own), bank officials become more friendly and eager to please. If you have a net worth of $50,000, excluding your own house and personal possessions, you can expect a bank manager to make an effort to greet you by name, and you will most likely be able to get a personal loan of up to $10,000 with just your signature. If your net worth is $100,000, you may start meeting a few executives from the main office, and $25,000 will not be too high at all for a personal loan on just a signature. At $250,000 you can expect to know an officer in a friendly way, say on the golf course, and $50,000 will not be too high regardless of the interest rates or tightness of money. At half a million, a vice president, particularly of a smaller bank, will want to be your friend, and $100,000 will be available on your signature. And so on.

Savings and Loan Institutions

Savings and loans put most of their money on real estate—this is their primary source of investment—so they are an excellent source of financing, whether the property you are buying is high-priced or low. Savings and loans finance condominiums and shopping centers, skyscrapers and apartment buildings—everything that involves real estate is their domain. While the maximum percentage of appraised value a savings and loan can loan is set by law, the interest rate and the points charged vary with each institution and it pays to shop around. The easiest way of doing this is to simply get the telephone book and look under savings and loan institutions, then call each one, ask for a loan officer, and describe the type of mortgage you want. I have never encountered a case where such an officer would not tell the best rate and point out discounts his savings and loan currently had available.

Savings and loans also fund FHA and GI loans, and in addition they make a loan called a PMI, (to be discussed below), under which they can loan up to 95 percent of the appraised value. Savings and loan institutions do not normally, however, make personal loans, and your signature without the collateral of a piece of property will get you nowhere here. It may be helpful to refer to Table 5-4, which lists the typical differences between banks and savings and loan institutions with regard to real estate loans.

Table 5-4. Real Estate Loans: Banks versus Savings and Loans

Banks usually can loan up to a maximum of 90% of appraised value, but normally try to stay below 80%. Federal savings and loans can loan up to 95% on private mortgage-insured loans.

Banks and savings and loans normally do not make loans on bare land (although banks will make personal loans which might then be used to purchase bare land.)

Banks tend to be stiffer in their requirements for the borrower. Where the savings and loan is usually most interested in the property, the bank is interested equally in the property and the borrower. Banks usually require an income of 4½ times the monthly payment (with no debts running for more than 6 months). Savings and loans may require a 4 to 1 ratio.

Savings and loans are geared to handle foreclosures because the majority of their business comes from real estate loans. Banks are not geared to handle real estate foreclosures.

Savings and loans generally charge 6 months prepayment penalty or 2% of the loan balance anytime the loan is paid off before it comes due. Banks have the same prepayment charges, but often waive them after the loan has been in force for 5 or 6 years.

Savings and loans may often be ¼ to ½ of a percent lower in interest rates than banks—this helps them generate real estate loans. In hard times, however, it is the savings and loans which run out of money to loan first. Banks may charge higher interest rates, but usually have plenty of money available.

Banks tend to be more conservative and savings and loans more liberal about real estate loans.

REITs

Real estate investment trusts (REITs) are a major source of construction-loan money in the country, particularly where large developments are concerned. They operate in this manner: Say a builder wants to borrow a million dollars to construct a shopping center. A bank or a savings and loan may be willing to loan him money once the project is completed but may not be willing to loan money during the construction period. The reason for this is risk. Anything can happen to a building (and often does) during construction—labor strikes can halt or cripple work, fire can destroy the structure, death of the contractor can halt construction, and so on. Unless the builder is strong enough to borrow the money on his personal credit, which in most cases he is not, he cannot effectively put the property up as collateral and does not get the loan, from a bank. A REIT, however, is a strong financial institution. It goes to a bank or savings and loan and borrows money at the prime rate on its own credit and then lends it to the builder, charging anywhere from 4 to 5 percent above the prime rate as its profit for running the risks. Borrowing millions in this way, many builders have succeeded in creating enormous projects that would otherwise have never gotten started. Of course, the interest rate to the developer is enormous. If the prime is 7, he has to pay 4 higher at a minimum, or 11 percent. If the prime is 11 or 12 or higher, he can end up paying 15 or 16 percent interest on his construction loan. Few builders can afford this kind of money, and REITs went into a slump in the early seventies, largely because new builders could not afford their price and old builders could not keep up and were foreclosed upon. (For a discussion of how to buy into REITs, see Chapter 6.)

Mortgage Bankers

A mortgage banker is basically a company that goes out and gets the right kind of loan for you, the borrower. There are literally hundreds in virtually every state, and many national concerns. If you want a construction loan from a REIT, if you want an FHA or GI loan, if you want a PMI (to be discussed shortly), the mortgage banker. is there. And usually his interest rates and points are highly competitive. He makes much of his money by servicing the loan. Servicing works in this way. Say a borrower obtains an FHA loan from a mortgage banker. The banker does not fund the money. Instead, he goes to a savings and loan or bank and gets them to put up the money, then he charges the lender a fee to collect the payments each month from the borrower. In this way banks on the East Coast can make loans on the West Coast without opening offices there—they place them through mortgage bankers already established on the West Coast. Similarly, Western lenders can make loans in this manner in the East. Ten years ago a mortgage banker would get 2 percent of the loan for servicing it—a healthy fee. But competition and the rapid expansion of banks and savings and loans have dropped that fee down to about 0.6 percent. This figure is close to forcing many mortgage bankers out of business. But while they remain, they are a useful source of funds.

Any listing of mortgage bankers would necessarily leave out important ones, since there are many hundreds. The easiest way to find them is the same method used to check banks or savings and loans. Simply look up mortgage bankers in the telephone book and call to find current interest rates and points.

Life Insurance Companies

Life insurance companies are an enormous source of real estate financing; however, except in two kinds of cases, the individual usually cannot take direct advantage of them. Insurance companies will make all types of loans, but they usually place them through mortgage bankers. A few insurance companies, such as Prudential, have of late opened their own loan offices, where individuals can obtain loans, but this has not been a common practice. Further, Prudential, through its public mortgage offices across the country, will make loans only of a million dollars or more. They will not usually make home mortgage loans to individuals. The other method of using insurance companies is to borrow money on your life insurance. A bank or your insurance agent can tell if you qualify for this. Many people have gotten their start in real estate by borrowing the down payment on their life insurance.

Private Individuals

There was a time a few years ago when private lenders were looked down upon. They were thought of as something akin to loan sharks. But with today's enormous interest rates this has changed. Today private lenders are a much sought-after source of money. Often their rates are lower than other lenders, and they have money immediately available to loan. A private lender is anyone who will loan money who is not a lending institution such as a bank or savings and loan. The biggest problem with private lenders is finding them.

Probably the best source of obtaining private financing is by means of an advertisement in the financial section of the local paper. (Private lenders sometimes advertise here also.) Advertisements frequently appear which simply read like this: "Need $100,000—will give first (or second) mortgage on well-secured apartment building—rates must be competitive." People with money to loan read the financial pages and will call. However, when dealing with an individual, you had better know what you are doing. Unlike an institution, the individual has little public image to maintain, and if you give him the opportunity to take advantage of your ignorance, he may do it— perhaps with a clause creating a balloon payment slipped in here or a clause tying up your personal as well as your real property slipped in there. If you do not know enough to protect yourself and want to deal with a private lender, a good idea is to do it through a broker. (Brokers are also good sources of private money, particularly those who advertise that they are "mortgage brokers.")

The broker usually takes a fee of 1 to 2 points for his services, which is usually paid by the borrower. On a $10,000 loan that can be $100 to $200—a small fee when you consider the grief that can be avoided by having someone experienced with loans handle the deal.

Wraparounds

This type of financing has been available for years, but is now coming into vogue because of enormously high interest rates. It is a type of creative financing that allows the borrower to combine two loans, one for an older and lower interest rate and one for a newer and higher rate. It works this way:

Let us assume that you are a buyer purchasing a $150,000 apartment building, putting $50,000 down. This means that you will need a mortgage of $100,000. The interest rate on such a mortgage could be anywhere from 8 to 12 percent (or higher), depending on the financial conditions at the time. Let us arbitrarily say that the interest rate is 10 percent. That is a hefty rate of interest to pay and can make your payments quite high. You decide that you simply cannot afford to buy at 10 percent, and you start to look for a way around the high rate. You discover that the current owner of the apartment building has an $80,000 loan on it that was taken out several years ago, and the interest rate is only 6 percent. You check with the loan company that holds this mortgage and discover that they will be happy to let you assume it; they only require that as part of the assumption the interest rate be raised to 10 percent! You have gotten nowhere, right? Wrong. Now is the time for you to create a wraparound loan. You go to another lender (or it could be the owner if he is willing to carry the loan himself) and ask for a $20,000 loan at 12 percent, explaining you want it to "wrap around" the present $80,000 loan. You will make payments direct to this lender on the total borrowed sum of $100,000, at 6 percent on the first $80,000 and 12 percent on the balance. He will then take out the amount due on his $20,000 and make the monthly payments on the $80,000 loan himself. You will have low interest on the major portion of your financing, the new lender will have 12 percent (higher than the going rate), and the old lender will continue receiving payments on his loan at 6 percent.

The wraparound is similar to a second loan on the property, with this important difference. In a second, you the owner control who gets paid and when. In a wraparound, the second lender has complete control over the first loan. If you fail to make a payment, he is the first to know it, and this gives him much greater flexibility in the event of a foreclosure. He charges the additional 1 or 2 percent above the going rate on his money (the $20,000 sum) for the added risk; after all this loan is still not as good as a straight first.

Two problems are often encountered when getting a wraparound. The first is that not all lenders will make them. Unless you know a bank manager or official, you do not have a chance of getting such financing from a commercial bank. The run-of-the-mill loan officer will laugh such a proposal out of his office. On the other hand, savings and loan institutions and mortgage bankers that handle such creative financing with regularity might be much more accepting. If you want this sort of financing, you will have to shop around to get it.

The second problem is a small item called an *alienation clause* that is occasionally included in first loans. (It is almost always included in second loans.) An alienation clause simply states that if the person the loan is given to sells the property, the loan must immediately be paid in full. If the first loan of $80,000 in our last example contained such a clause, the deal could not be made. As soon as the seller signed away the property, the $80,000 would be due and payable regardless of who was deemed responsible for the monthly payments. What to do when you discover an alienation clause? About the only thing you can do is to ask the holder of the mortgage to waive the clause. There is a chance he will do this, but there is a bigger chance he will not.

Consider again the case of our lender who has the $80,000 mortgage on the property, only this time assume he has an alienation clause. You, the borrower come to him and ask him to waive it. This is what he is going to think: If he waives it, he gains nothing. If he refuses and you go ahead and buy anyhow, the loan gets paid off. He gets back his $80,000 which was loaned out at 6 percent, and he can turn around and reloan it at the current rate of 10 percent. He can potentially make an additional 4 percent on his money just by refusing to waive the clause. If you were the lender, what would you do?

Credit Unions, Credit Agencies, and Pension Funds

Credit unions are an excellent source of funds at reasonable rates if you are a member. If you are not, try some other source. Often credit unions will lend primarily on the basis of the borrower's standing *within the union* and the value of the property. Consequently, borrowers with somewhat tarnished track records or credit who have good credit-union standing can get their best loans here.

Pension funds are an excellent source of real estate loans if your project is large enough. Usually they will not touch anything under $100,000, and large funds will not go below $1 million. It is simply economically unfeasible for them to do so. A good mortgage broker can put you in touch with numerous funds if your project is big enough.

Credit agencies, occasionally called finance companies, are a last source of real estate loans..They are useful if you have to have money and cannot get it anywhere else, but you have to pay their price. Interest rates of 18 percent even in good times are not uncommon here. Most credit agencies do not make first loans. Normally, when you can offer a lender a first loan, you go to one of the institutions we have previously considered. But there may come a time when you need to borrow on one piece of property to buy another and you already have a first loan on it and perhaps even a second. A credit agency is your last, best hope.

These agencies generally make loans that are secured by a combination of personal and real property. What this means is that in the event you fail to pay, the lender, usually at *his* option, can take back the property *or* tie up all your banking funds, your furniture and clothes, your car, etc., until you make payment. Besides paying higher rates of interest for this type of loan, you are also putting up a lot more collateral.

PRIVATE MORTGAGE-INSURED LOANS

Private mortgage-insured loans (PMIs) are an old type of loan that has had a resurgence in recent years. They are simply conventional loans with insurance on them from private insuring companies. They work like FHA and VA loans (although they are not connected with the government).

When a borrower applies for a PMI loan from, for example, a savings and loan institution, the savings and loan forwards the application to a special mortgage insurance company. (Mortgage Guaranty Insurance Corp.—MGIC—is currently the largest.) The insurance company either accepts or rejects the borrower. It the borrower is accepted and the loan is made, the insurance company usually guarantees the payment of the first 25 percent of the amount borrowed. Suppose Mr. Jones borrows $20,000 on a PMI loan and after one year defaults. The lender has to foreclose, but his loss is not $20,000. It is 25 percent less, or only $15,000. PMIs then, are simply a form of insurance the lender can buy to protect his loan.

While the insurance only covers the first 25 percent of the loss (or 20 percent if the lender wishes a reduced amount), this is money that is in the greatest-risk area. In our example, if the lender has to sell Mr. Jones's property, chances are he might get back $16,000 to $19,000 in hard times. But the chance that he would get back less than $15,000, or three-fourths of the loan amount, in the event of a foreclosure sale is remote; hence, lenders are most happy to make PMI loans.

The interest rate on PMIs is the same as the current rate on any conventional first mortgage. The largest source for them is the savings and loan industry. Usually there are no more than 1 or 1½ points to pay on a PMI, and, best of all for the borrower, they can be made for as high as 95 percent of the appraised value.

But before you rush out to obtain one on your next purchase, keep these warnings in mind. PMIs are not for everyone. When the Federal Home Loan Bank Board authorized federal savings and loan institutions to lend money on PMIs (before that, banks and mortgage bankers were the only sources), it set $30,000 as the maximum loan. In addition, there are almost no lenders who make PMI loans on apartment buildings, trailer parks, or other income property. PMIs, then, are for the *home buyer* in the price range below a $30,000 loan amount.

Also, although savings and loans can loan up to 95 percent of the appraised value, they can only do it after the mortgage insuring company approves the borrower. Like any other insurance company, private mortgage insurers will only lend to people who are financially "well." It is fair to say that although a PMI is about the *best* loan you can get when you are buying a house, it is also about the *hardest* to get. In general, you have to be making *at least* four times the monthly payment, you can have almost *no* adverse items on your credit report, and you have to have a *perfect* track record. Here is the profile of a typical buyer (Table 5-5).

As you can see, both buyer and property have to be first rate before a PMI can be obtained. If you are first rate, you can apply for a PMI from the closest savings and loan, mortgage banker, or bank.

In general, the closing costs on conventional loans are the same as for government loans with this exception: whether buyer or seller pays any particular item, such as points or credit report or title insurance policy, is strictly up to agreement or local custom. This is unlike, for example, FHA loans, on which the government insists that the purchaser pay no more than 1 point.

This is the financing available in today's market. The interest rates tend to be high, and money tends to be scarce. But if the borrower is

Table 5-5. Some Conditions That Must Normally Be Met for a Buyer to Obtain a New PMI

1. The buyer must qualify at least 4½ to 1 (occasionally 4 to 1 is allowed on a case-by-case determination).

2. All income that cannot be verified in the usual manner (employer's statement) must be backed up by W-2 forms or income tax returns.

3. Stable employment for a minimum of 3 years must be shown, and if frequent job changes are indicated, each job change should show a higher salary and responsibility.

4. All debts of more than 90 days (from date of credit report) must be itemized and counted for income-debt-ratio purposes.

5. Calculating the income ratio (see no. 1 above)—altogether, monthly payments including taxes, insurance, and private insurance premiums plus all debts of this amount must not be more than 25% of the borrower's income. (The short-term debts must not exceed 33% of the total debts.)

6. The buyer should have no bankruptcies or collection problems.

7. Any credit problems should have reasonable explanations; more than one or two derogatory items may cause rejection.

8. No second mortgages are permitted.

9. Ideally the borrower should be the married head of a household. Preference is usually given to those who exhibit excellent income and payment stability.

creative, spends some time shopping around, and knows what is available, there is almost nothing that cannot be done. To further aid you, here are Tables 5-6, 5-7, 5-8, and 5-9, which I am sure you will find most useful.

SELLING REAL ESTATE IN A TIGHT MONEY MARKET

One other area needs to be dealt with, and that is the problems that sellers (and buyers) encounter when they try to sell real estate during an inflation when money is extremely difficult to borrow. It is rarely the case that someone will have all cash to put up for a piece of property; more often a loan as part of the purchase price is required. If, because of inflation, banks and savings and loans are not willing to loan money, it may not be possible to make a sale.

Table 5-6. Monthly Payments for Each $1,000 You Borrow

To use chart or figure the cost each month of a mortgage, find the payment period and the interest rate appropriate to your loan. Then multiply the number shown by thousands of dollars borrowed:

Interest rate (percent)	Payment period				
	10 years	15 years	20 years	25 years	30 years
5	$10.61	$ 7.91	$6.60	$5.85	$5.37
5½	10.86	8.18	6.88	6.15	5.68
6	11.11	8.44	7.17	6.45	6.00
6½	11.36	8.72	7.46	6.76	6.33
7	11.62	8.99	7.76	7.07	6.66
7½	11.88	9.28	8.06	7.39	7.00
8	12.14	9.56	8.37	7.72	7.34
8½	12.40	9.85	8.68	8.06	7.69
9	12.67	10.15	9.00	8.40	8.05
9½	12.94	10.45	9.33	8.74	8.41
10	13.22	10.75	9.66	9.09	8.78

SOURCE: U.S. Department of Agriculture, Agricultural Research Service, Consumer and Food Economic Division, Home and Garden Bulletin 182, December 1970. 0-397-411.

Table 5-7. Effect of Size of Down Payment on Cost of a $20,000 Home, with Interest at 9 Percent

Down payment	Monthly payment (principal and interest)			Total interest		
	20 years	25 years	30 years	20 years	25 years	30 years
$ 0	$180	$168	$161	$23,160	$30,220	$37,820
500	176	164	157	22,580	29,460	36,880
1,000	171	160	153	22,000	28,710	35,930
2,000	162	151	145	29,850	27,200	34,040
3,000	153	143	137	19,690	25,690	32,150
4,000	144	134	129	18,530	24,180	30,260
5,000	135	126	121	17,370	22,670	28,370

NOTE: Monthly payment rounded to nearest $1; total interest rounded to nearest $10.
SOURCE: U.S. Department of Agriculture, Agricultural Research Service, Consumer and Food Economic Division, Home and Garden Bulletin 182, December 1970. 0-397-411.

Table 5-8. Effect of Repayment Period on Cost of a $20,000 Loan at 9 Percent

Payment period (years)	Monthly payment (principal and interest)	Total interest
5	$415	$ 4,910
10	253	10,400
15	203	16,490
20	180	23,160
25	168	30,220
30	161	37,820

NOTE: Monthly payment rounded to nearest $1; total interest rounded to nearest $10.

SOURCE: U.S. Department of Agriculture, Agricultural Research Service, Consumer and Food Economic Division, Home and Garden Bulletin 182, December 1970. 0-397-411.

Table 5-9. Effect of Interest Rate on Cost of a $20,000 Loan over a 25-Year Period

Interest rate (percent)	Monthly payment (principal and interest)	Total interest (over 25 years)
6	$129	$18,600
6½	135	20,440
7	141	22,390
7½	148	24,330
8	154	26,280
8½	161	28,200
9	168	30,220
9½	175	32,370
10	182	34,460

NOTE: Monthly payment rounded to nearest $1; total interest rounded to nearest $10.

SOURCE: U.S. Department of Agriculture, Agricultural Research Service, Consumer and Food Economic Division, Home and Garden Bulletin 182, December 1970. 0-397-411.

There are, of course, tried and true methods of dealing with this problem. Check *all* the lending institutions in an area including private lenders. But what if all sources run dry?

If the property is large, say, worth over $1 million, there are several alternatives. One is participation loans, wherein the lender obtains part ownership as part payment for lending the money. Another is wraparound financing, where upon a sale, a new loan encloses but does not pay off an old one, and the benefits of the old loan, such as low interest and low payments, remain. If you have a million-dollar piece of property, a mortgage banker can most likely steer you to an appropriate lender.

If you have a small residential piece of property, say a $30,000 home, the outlook is somewhat more bleak—but not hopeless. If the loan you have on your property does not contain an alienation clause (for it not to would be most unlikely, it should be noted), you can sell "subject to," like the "big boy" with the million-dollar property just described. (See "Wraparounds" for a complete discussion of this method.) If, however, your loan contains the standard alienation clause, in almost all cases (except government-insured loans) the lender would require you to pay off the loan along with a hefty prepayment penalty anytime you sell the property.

Let us take a typical case. A property owner with a $30,000 home has an existing $20,000 loan on it at 6 percent interest. He wants to sell, but the lender will not let anyone take over that loan. Rather, that loan has to be paid off, and a new one at the highest current interest rate, say 10 percent, has to be taken out. Further, because inflation is high and money is tight, the lender says that it will not give even a new 10 percent loan to just anyone—the buyer has to be grade AAA. What is the seller to do if he cannot find a grade AAA buyer, which is a real possibility?

Until late 1974 the seller had little choice but to scout around and try to find another lender, a virtual impossibility, *or* come up with a buyer who could pay the whole $30,000 in cash. However, at the end of last year in California a landmark decision was handed down by that state's Supreme Court. The court ruled, in effect, that the alienation clause which required the loan to become "due on" sale of the house was ineffective even if written into the loan *if* the property sold under an installment contract of sale.

An installment contract of sale is merely a contract wherein the seller agrees to sell his property at a specific future date. It has been used, in the past, when a buyer did not have enough money for a full down payment. The contract of sale would be executed, then the buyer would make regular installment payments until he had accumulated a full down payment, and then the transfer of deed would be made. Such an arrangement is a sort of combination lay-away plan and second mortgage. (For a more complete explanation see Chapter 9, discussion of land sales.)

The effect of the new decision is that the seller of virtually any house with an existing low-interest-rate mortgage can keep that mortgage on the house for use by a prospective buyer, provided he sells under an installment contract of sale. The buyer does not *assume* the old loan, but purchases the property *subject* to it. This means that at the end of the contract period (which can be for virtually any length of time) the buyer will still have to get a new first loan. But he hopes that by then interest rates will be down and money easier to get.

Although this type of financing is currently just available in California, decisions such as this, once made, often sweep across other states. A query to your local broker, lawyer, or real estate board should let you know whether it is in effect in your area.

FLEXIBLE INTEREST RATE MORTGAGES

When the "tight money" crunch hit in 1974, probably the most severely affected lenders were the savings and loan associations. Suddenly the interest rates on mortgages were at 11 percent, yet the vast majority of their loan portfolios were at around 6 or 7 percent, and they were locked into these loans for thirty years. To prevent such a financial strain from happening again, many associations have gone to a *variable interest rate mortgage*.

Quite simply, such a mortgage has only one basic feature that differs from all other kinds of mortgages: the interest rate goes up or down according to economic conditions. As of this writing, virtually all savings and loan associations that offer this loan tie it to the Federal Home Loan Bank Board Index. This is an index put out by the government which measures the cost of the money lenders borrow from the government. As the cost of borrowing money increases to them, they pass the increase on to the home mortgagor. Since the index comes out twice yearly, increases or reductions in interest rates are normally made every six months, and many associations write a clause into their loans providing a maximum rise or fall in interest rates of 2½ percent for the life of the loan.

Lenders point out certain advantages in variable interest rate mortgages to the borrowers. In many cases the loans are fully assumable by a new buyer, provided he qualifies. In most cases they provide a waiver of the prepayment penalty if the loan is paid off within ninety days of any interest rate increase.

As of this writing, only state savings and loan associations are offering variable interest rate mortgages. However, there is legislation pending before Congress to allow federally chartered associations to also offer such loans. In addition, other legislation would allow lenders to add the amount of an increase in the interest rate to the term of the loan thus keeping payments constant.

The disadvantages of the variable interest rate loan to the borrower are obvious: the interest rate and consequently the monthly payment might rise unexpectedly some time during the life of the loan. The advantages, however, are not as clearly seen. Of course, the rate and monthly payment might drop, but beyond that, this type of loan makes lenders more willing to loan money during hard times. After all, what good is a fixed interest rate mortgage, as we have had, if nobody will make any loans?

6

How to Invest in Groups

Thus far we have been concerned with the individual who sets out to make large profits in real estate alone (or in a husband and wife team). But there are many individuals who realize the enormous potential for profit in real estate but for a variety of reasons do not want to become personally involved. They would prefer to invest their money in real estate in much the same way people invest in stocks or bonds—simply put up so much money and at the end of the year get something like a dividend check showing profits.

Today it is possible to invest in real estate this way. While I feel the profits on such investments are not likely to be nearly as high, these are "clean" deals. By this I mean that the investor does not have to "get his hands dirty" by going through the work of buying and selling property and maintaining or improving it. He joins a group of other investors, and they hire someone else to do the work. Or, as is usually the case, they "hire" the originator of the group. Typically a group is started by someone who has a notion to buy some real estate, say an apartment house, but who does not have enough capital. He rounds up some of his friends or, on a larger scale, sends out a prospectus to thousands of individuals. Those who "buy in," or invest their money, agree to let the promoter manage the project for a fee. Usually this comes off the top before profits come out. In a good group investment there is enough money to pay the promoter and show a profit for everyone concerned. In a bad one, usually only the promoter makes money.

Before looking at the two major types of group investments in real estate available today, let us consider briefly some of the *advantages* group ownership offers.

Let us assume that you do not wish to use the Home Reinvestment Plan outlined in Chapter 2. Perhaps you are not willing to make the sacrifices it demands. For example, you do not want to change homes often or you do not want to buy a home *strictly* as an investment. Yet, you do want to invest in real estate. Aside from management one of the biggest problems you are likely to face is the limited amount of capital you can raise.

If you are like most of us, you always seem to be just a few dollars short of the amount required to get that really great deal. For example, in Chapter 2 we considered the buying of trailer parks and apartment houses. I would say that an absolutely bare minimum of $10,000 (with a relatively safe figure closer to $25,000) would be needed to swing such a deal. That is not to say that this sum would be the purchase price—this would be the sum needed to swing a deal where the purchase price was four to five times this amount (or more if you were very fortunate in your financing).

While for some people $10,000 is not a large sum, for many it constitutes a good portion of life savings. For many others, it is simply more money than they have. The solution many people take is investment in a group.

When you invest in a group, you overcome the major problem involved with property investment, management. Most group investments have a *general partner* or *developer* who has put the members of the group in contact with each other and who presumably has the expertise to manage whatever property is being bought. This person may be, for example, a local real estate broker who wants to interest ten people in going together in the purchase of an apartment house. It may take a $25,000 down payment to buy the building, but with ten partners each would only have to invest $2,500. All would join the group with the understanding that the broker, for a fee, would manage the building after it was purchased. That way each investor would have a "clean deal." The only active part he would take would be to sign the group agreement and the check for his share. At year's end he would receive back a share of the profits or a notice of the amount of loss. He would never have to fix broken windows, answer tenant complaints, argue over utility bills, or live through the many other headaches that are involved in real estate management.

Many professional people such as doctors, lawyers, and accountants and many self-employed owners of businesses who see the advantages of investing in real estate opt for the group plan. The lack of management problems is usually their biggest single motive.

Another advantage of group purchase of real estate involves liability. Normally speaking, any time you take out a loan you assume responsibility for its eventual repayment. In the purchase of real estate this often holds true (though not always). When you purchase a building for $100,000 and put $25,000 down, you have one or more mortgages for $75,000 remaining, on which you make a regular monthly payment. If the building for one reason or another, say unusually high vacancy, fails to bring in the amount of money you have anticipated, you may not be able to make your monthly payments. The lender then takes the building back. We all know about foreclosure, even if it has never happened to us. It is the risk one takes any time a loan is obtained.

However, if you are unable to make your payments and the mortgagee, or lender, forecloses, you may face a further risk that many people are unaware of. Assuming the mortgagee is other than the former owner, his desire will undoubtedly be to get back his cash. He will want to sell the apartment to the highest bidder in order to get back his $75,000 loan (assuming you defaulted before your first payment and the loan balance is the same as before). If for some reason the building does not bring the full $75,000—for example, if you overpaid—you may be liable for the *deficiency*. If it only sells for $65,000, the lender may be able to secure a default judgement against you for $10,000. With this judgment he can tie up your bank account, home, other real estate, in fact all the other property you own, and force its sale to recoup his money.

If however, you purchase property through a group, in most cases *your liability is limited* to only that amount of money that you originally put up. Assuming that you are not the broker who organized the deal, if a $10,000 deficiency judgment were secured on an apartment-building foreclosure, as a *limited partner* in a group you normally would not be liable for any part of it. As a group member you can never lose more than you originally invested.

As a side note, many states have *purchase-money laws*. In simple terms, these provide that whatever money is borrowed on a piece of property such as an apartment building, if it is borrowed in order to *purchase* the property, is protected from a lender's deficiency judgment. Even if provisions for making up deficiencies are written into the promissory note, they are ineffective where this law operates.

One last word about risk is in order. Although most group investments limit liability, they are still a risky vehicle for the investor. When you put your money up in a group, you lose something besides headaches. You lose control. The promoter determines where the money will be spent and how.

SYNDICATION

The most popular vehicle for investing in a group today is the syndicate. Every time I hear the word I picture the Chicago mobster days of the twenties. It seemed, in those days, that one or another gangster who represented the "syndicate" was always trying to take over territory run by a rival mobster. Syndicates seemed to be responsible for bootlegging, loan sharking, and even the St. Valentine massacre. Obviously, in our discussion of real estate this is not the kind of syndication we are speaking of.

A "syndicate" can be broadly defined as any group of individuals who gather together for a specific business purpose. In a sense, a syndicate is like a "cartel." In terms of real estate, a syndicate is simply a group of individuals who get together for the purpose of purchasing property.

Private Offering

While syndication laws vary from state to state, a most common form of syndication is the *private offering*. An individual, quite often a real estate broker or a builder, will want to purchase a large development, say a shopping center. In order to raise the capital, he will approach several friends and offer them part of the deal. Say the center will cost $400,000 and will require $100,000 down. He has $10,000, so he goes to nine friends and tries to get each to put up $10,000. (A limit of ten members to a private offering is not uncommon, often as a result of state laws.) In some states the number of "friends" he can approach is limited by law. In California, for example, he cannot approach more than 25 people. Unfortunately, it is virtually impossible to regulate this requirement, and in actual practice promoters may often ask many more than the set number before they finally get ten to put up, in terms of our example, the $10,000 apiece.

Assuming the promoter does get his nine other people, he next has them sign a limited-partnership agreement. This usually states the amount of money that has been raised and how much each individual has put in, and it specifies how profits are to be paid out and how much of a fee the promoter will take for his services.

The danger with such agreements is that the investor often does not know if enough money is being raised to bring the deal to completion. In a syndication to build a shopping center, $100,000 from ten investors may be sought to go with a $300,000 loan to build a $400,000 project. As time passes and costs of building materials rise, the center may end up costing $450,000, necessitating an additional input of money by the investors. Or in the case of existing buildings, vacancies might be higher than expected, and again the investors could be asked to come up with additional cash to save their initial investment. And I have seen bad situations in private offerings where the property to be developed was initially described as such and such and the property finally purchased was considerably different. If things such as this happen and there is money lost, watch out for lawsuits against the promoter, who may be innocent. Good syndication deals will usually specify exactly the location and give comprehensive details of the type of property to be developed.

Finally, there is usually one person liable for the actions of the syndicate. In the private offering we have been using as an example, none of the nine friends who put up $10,000 apiece is liable for any loss other than this money. However, in contrast to a corporation, where no one at all is personally liable, in a limited partnership one person is personally liable and that is the promoter. He is technically the general partner, while all others are the limited partners.

Normally the private offering is not the kind of syndication you can go looking for; it has to find you. Most often brokers or accountants are aware of such groups and can have someone from them contact you. They are designed to be a coalition of friends, relatives, or associates who pool their resources toward a common goal, in this case real estate profit. Of course there is a verbal agreement, but always be sure to have a written agreement also—nothing breaks up friendships faster than trying to recall what was verbally agreed upon a year earlier. A private offering tends by its very nature to be informal. It is probably for this very reason that in most states they are not regulated (beyond such rules as approaching no more than twenty-five and having no more than ten members). There is no investigation by a public organization to determine whether the projected development is a good deal or a bad one, not even to see if it is in fact the same deal as the promoter represents it to be. The limited partners have no such protection, and theoretically they do not need it because only friends are involved. Because of the lack of government supervision, if you are involved in a private offering and you do not personally know the promoter (general partner), you had better know someone else who does, and very well. These are friendship deals, and if you are not a friend beforehand, you could be in trouble.

Public Offering

Public offerings are a different type of syndication, the sort commonly advertised. Usually they have a prospectus, which is a document of one or more pages that describes the partnership and the project. It normally would give the names, background, and assets of all the general partners (assuming there was more than one) and would give the exact location and description of the property. Before small public offerings of under one hundred investors can be sold to the public, they must usually be registered with a real estate or corporation commission. In many states an investigation is conducted by one or more such branches of government, and a judgment is reached on the basis of whether or not the proposed syndicate is "fair and equitable" to the public. If fraud or misrepresentation is discovered, such governmental bodies may prevent the public sale of the syndicate. (Note: Not all states are equally strict in their control of syndications.) You are likely to find a public syndication offering at an investment brokerage house or even simply advertised in local newspapers.

If a large public offering is made interstate, that is, all across the Eastern seaboard or on the West Coast or even nationwide, permission normally must be obtained from the Securities and Exchange Commission (SEC). These are probably the most rigorously investigated public offerings, though not necessarily the best deals. There are costs of as much as $50,000 involved in getting SEC clearance, and the time involved may drag into years.

Let us for a moment turn to the viewpoint of the promoter. The promoter of a limited partnership has the opportunity to expand his real estate interests and investments beyond his wildest dreams. There are no limits to the number of syndications he can arrange. A quick promoter can syndicate an apartment house, then quickly turn around and use the profits he derives from it to syndicate a commercial building, then a gas station, and so on. Each time he is putting up little or no money of his own, but each time he receives a fee for management as well as a share of the profits. The general rule seems to be that as long as he is successful, he has no trouble finding investors who will follow (even over a financial cliff). Before you rush out to become a syndicator, however, take note of two important facts. First, the syndication promoter must be above all a salesman—he has to convince large numbers of people to risk their money with him. Usually this means prior successful experience he can point to and large personal assets he can use to demonstrate that he is not in the deal for "a quick buck." Second, the syndication promoter must have a thorough knowledge of all the legal ramifications of limited-partnership law in his area. (The reader should note that the material in this book and particularly in this chapter is not a prospectus. It is in no way an offer or solicitation to sell or buy any securities and should not be considered sales literature. No governmental agency has reviewed any of this material.)

Tax Shelters

We have considered the advantages of joining a syndicate as a limited partner—more capital, no management headaches, and limited liability. There is one other reason why people invest in syndicates—to gain a tax shelter. Quite often professionals in the 50 percent plus bracket, that is, making about $60,000 a year, are the people who are most interested in syndications for this reason. In addition to providing *tax-free cash* in their pockets at year-end, many syndications can offer the advantage of showing a loss, sometimes of considerable proportions, that can be used to offset other income. (See Chapter 8 for a further explanation.)

This works much the same way as in Chapter 2 in the case of Gail and Howard VanTill, who were able to show a loss on the first year of ownership of their 28-unit apartment building and use that loss to offset their profits on the sale of their house on Justin Street. They deducted from their income all the interest on their mortgage, the depreciation on the building, the taxes, the maintenance, and so on, and they came up with a negative income, or in other words a loss. To see how this applies to syndication let us take the fictional example of a commercial building on a street we shall call Market Street. Jerold Hopkins is presented with the following statement when he is asked to join a private offering:

DESCRIPTION:
    Property—a large commercial building on the 1300 block of Market Street containing twenty-one shops

COST	
Down payment	$500,000
	$100,000
First loan at 9%	$300,000
Second loan at 10%	$100,000

INCOME:

Gross rents from all shops	$100,000 per year
Less vacancy factor (20%)	$ 20,000
Less operating expenses (20%)	$ 20,000
Net income	$ 60,000

EXPENSES:

Mortgage payment on first loan	$ 25,000
Mortgage payment on second loan	9,000
Taxes	20,000
	$ 54,000
Income	$ 60,000
Less expenses	54,000
Profit	$ 6,000

TAX EVALUATION:

Income		$60,000
Less mortgage interest on two loans, approx.	$ 30,000	
Less taxes	20,000	
Less depreciation (building worth estimated $400,000 written off at 125% per year for twenty years)	25,000	
Less personal-property depreciation (light fixtures, display cases, etc.)	12,000	87,000
Tax loss		$27,000

The syndicate is purchasing a half-million-dollar building. It is borrowing $400,000 on two loans and needs to provide $100,000 in cash. It is a private offering seeking ten investors to put up $10,000 apiece. For putting up this much money it offers the following:

First, after taking into account management (operating expenses), vacancy factors, payments on both mortgages and taxes, the building will show a profit of $6,000. Each investor will receive back $600 in cash the first year. However, this is not the kind of cash that you add to your taxable income in April. This is tax-free income. Quickly look at the part of the statement which shows tax evaluation and note that after paying off interest, taxes, and depreciation the building shows a loss, not a profit. You do not pay taxes on a loss, even if it puts money in your pocket!

In addition, the loss on the building during the projected first year exceeds the income by $27,000. This means that each investor has one-tenth of $27,000 that he can apply as loss to his other regular income. (Note: For possible changes in this law see the section on tax problems in Chapter 8.) If an investor's other income is $60,000 on which he is paying a 50 percent tax, he can now reduce that income by $2,700 to $57,300. Since he has been paying 50 percent tax, this means a tax saving to him of half the $2,700, or $1,350—cash in his pocket. When we add the $1,350 in tax-saving cash to the $600, we find that an investor of $10,000 who is in the 50 percent tax bracket will receive back $1,950 in spendable cash income (no tax to pay on this money) the first year, or a return of better than 19 percent. Is it any wonder that thousands of people have flocked to join syndications?

Yes it is. A smart investor would not invest in this building.

A smart investor looking at the statement would realize that 20 percent is very low for operating expenses. Normally 40 to 45 percent is used. If we figure 42 percent, this deducts an additional $22,000 from the gross income of $100,000. Since profit (expenses minus income) on the building is shown as only $6,000, we can expect the building will actually show a loss of $16,000 the first year.

In addition, any good commercial building will have a vacancy factor that is down around 10 percent or less. Think of all the outstanding commercial buildings you have been in, the successful ones. How many empty shops do you see? Very few. Why does this building project a 20 percent vacancy factor? Could it be that there are hidden elements in the deal that the promoter is not revealing, such as harsh competition or a poor area? Another potential minus of the offering. (It could be a plus, of course, if the promoter is just being cautious.)

I chose this particular illustration to show why so many syndications have "gone on the rocks" in the past two years. The investors in many of these bad deals were lured in on the basis of a tax shelter. But the developments themselves did not have the potential to show a profit. When inflation hit and the economy stagnated, projects that were operating on a thin margin (such as this one with a potential real profit of – $16,000) found that losses were staggering. In our example, this might mean that each investor would have to come up with $1,600 more the first year. Imagine what would happen to this investment if twice the estimated number of shops closed, making the actual vacancy factor 40 percent. (Note: This means that 60 percent of the building is still occupied.) Just a 10 percent additional vacancy factor takes away one-tenth of the gross income of $100,000, or $10,000. Since there is no profit to offset this, each of the ten investors will have to come up with an additional $1,000 just to keep the project alive.

But what if vacancies soar to 50 percent, as has happened in some buildings in the past few years? Disaster for the investor who put in $10,000 the first year and got another bill for anywhere from $1,600 on up. (Of course he is writing this off taxes, so each dollar of loss is still only 50¢ in a 50 percent tax bracket.) But chances are that in such a deal, many of the investors will refuse to come up with more money. Any investor who wants to stick it out must make up their losses as well as his own. Usually nobody comes up with more money and foreclosure is the result. The investor in the 50 percent tax bracket usually deducts all his investment, giving him a $5,000 tax savings, but he invested $10,000. This is not the smart man's way to make money.

This has happened in so many cases over the past few years that syndication has gotten a bad name. Actually, investors mainly have only themselves to blame. An old rule of thumb about tax-sheltered investments is, "If the project is not economically sound, don't invest. Never buy anything just for a tax shelter." There are many excellent syndications that have continuously shown an actual profit. If you are thinking of buying into a limited-partnership syndication, reread this chapter. Make sure that you buy an economically good investment.

There is one additional restriction on a syndication that should be noted. In late 1974, the Internal Revenue Service in a statement of procedure indicated that if an investor can deduct in the first two years of operation more than he put into the venture in the first place, the IRS would no longer consider the entire syndication a tax shelter. The ruling was apparently intended to hit the "front end" deals which had been promising 100 percent plus tax shelters and which, incidentally, were among the shakiest of such ventures.

REITS (REAL ESTATE INVESTMENT TRUSTS)

These are the "cleanest" of all real estate investments. The investor need only buy stock in a REIT and collect his dividends each quarter. REITs have been appropriately termed the mutual funds of real estate.

Essentially, a REIT is a pooling of resources by a vast number of investors. It works much in the same manner as a corporation. You buy into a REIT by purchasing shares. Each share yields a certain profit. If there is a loss, however, no investor is required to make it good. As in syndicates, the liability is limited to the initial amount of money put up.

REITs came into their own with the Real Estate Investment Trust Act of 1960. The importance of this act is that it exempts the earnings of REITs from federal income tax, provided they meet certain very specific requirements. These are the following: First, the company must distribute 90 percent or more of its net income to its stockholders. Second, at least 75 percent of a REIT's income must come from real estate business, though the trust cannot participate directly in the operation or management of its holdings. Finally, the Internal Revenue Code has said that no more than 30 percent of gross receipts can be derived from capital gain.

The advantage a REIT has over an ordinary corporation is in taxation. Ordinarily a corporation must first pay 52 percent of its net profits in taxes; then it distributes the rest to its shareholders, who must pay regular tax on it. The income has been taxed *twice*. A REIT, as mentioned, pays no income tax on its profits. It distributes them directly to its shareholders, who then pay either regular tax or capital gains tax (usually a much smaller amount) on them. In a REIT the investor pays taxes only once.

There are basically two kinds of REITs, *mortgage trusts* and *equity trusts*. A mortgage trust gets its income chiefly from interest on long- and short-term loans on real estate projects. In other words, the investor buys shares, and the REIT uses the money received from the shares plus money it borrows to issue new loans. The interest it receives back on these is paid out to the investor as profit. An equity trust works in a slightly different fashion. It uses the investor's money to purchase property. Then it leases out the property and receives rental income on it which is paid to the investor as profit.

As you can see, a REIT does virtually the same thing any individual investor can do for himself. However, for a management fee (which comes out before profits) it handles all the "dirty work." Over the past decade and a half, REITs have shown returns in the 8 to 10 percent bracket on money invested. With the coming of the modern recession, however, REIT performance has slipped somewhat. Here is why.

In addition to loaning out the money that investors put into mortgage trusts, REITs got a large portion of their business from borrowing money at the prime interest rate (the amount banks charge their very best customers) and then loaning it out at a higher rate to developers, usually in the form of short-term construction loans. This worked out quite well as long as the prime interest rate remained low. At a 5 percent prime, the mortgage REIT could afford to borrow and make construction loans at 9 percent. The 4 percent margin took into account operational costs and the necessary risk involved in any construction loan. (The builder may not finish the project, and there is nothing harder to dispose of than a half-built building.) When the prime rate went to 9 percent and higher, however, the mortgage REITs found they could not make construction loans at anything less than 13 to 14 percent. At this much higher rate, builders simply could not afford to borrow the money. Mortgage REITs saw a great reduction in their volume of new business, in addition to a reduction in the amount of construction undertaken nationwide. And since their old business was primarily long-term loans lent out at earlier and lower interest, the return to investors dropped.

The equity REITs have fared somewhat better, since their income is derived from rent on lands. Their problem is that with the reduction in the building of new projects there are fewer and fewer new deals they can get into. Consequently their new business has suffered.

In the 1960s the REITs were one of the most promising of the "clean" real estate investments, offering regular returns from 8 to 9 percent. But since the beginning of this decade their promise has gone largely unfulfilled. Some have declared smaller profits, some have shown no profit at all. Today a good REIT may be a sound investment, but good REITs are hard to find. Note: There are nearly 200 REITs in the United States, and many are listed on the New York or American stock exchange. Any good stock broker can give you an accounting of the up-to-date profit picture on any particular REIT.

There is one last disadvantage of a REIT, and it becomes apparent when the REIT is compared to syndication. Remember that in a syndicate a tax shelter was passed on to the investor. Someone in the 50 percent tax bracket might make more money on the tax shelter his syndicate offered than on his cash return. This meant that profits of from 20 to 30 percent were possible and common.

A REIT provides no such tax shelter. Any accounting losses on property or loans that the REIT may have are absorbed entirely by the REIT and not passed on to the investor. In addition, whereas in a syndicate if you made $1,000 cash on a $10,000 investment the cash quite often was tax-free, in a REIT the same $1,000 would go into your pocket as regular income or capital gain and be subject to taxation. The person who was in the 50 percent tax bracket and performed so well in a syndicate does not come out well at all in a REIT. If the $1,000 profit is regular income, he must pay 50 percent of it as tax. The government gets $500 and he gets $500, cutting his actual return from 10 to 5 percent. If it is capital gains he declares only half, or $500, and then probably pays 50 percent on this, or $250, leaving his actual return at $750, or 7½ percent. Better, but still not much compared with syndication.

7

The "Repo" Market

When a house is lost through foreclosure, the new owner is the lender who gave the money for the original mortgage. In 99 percent of the cases, the lender is not in business to own property outright. He only wants to lend money on property and make his profit on the interest. When he acquires a house through foreclosure, it is a headache for him and he wants to sell it as soon as possible in order to get his money out so that he can loan it elsewhere. It is at this point that the "repo," or repossessed, market begins.

As mentioned earlier, during the dark days of the last great depression it was possible to buy repossessed houses and other types of property from banks at greatly reduced prices. The reason was as simple as supply and demand. Because of poor business conditions and enormous unemployment, the banks foreclosed on great numbers of houses, apartment buildings, and commercial buildings. But when they turned around and tried to sell them, they could find no buyers. Everyone was in the same boat—out of work and out of money. Consequently, the banks were forced to hold these properties and pay taxes on them. When some enterprising individual finally came along with a few dollars and a dream, the banks were happy to let these places go for far below their original market value. (Remember, in those days loans rarely were for more than 60 to 75 percent of value, so the bank could cut a fourth or more off the price and theoretically still not lose money.)

But the conditions of a depression do not hold during a recession. While selective unemployment and somewhat unhealthy business conditions do result in an increase in repossessions, there are usually enough individuals in healthy financial conditions to buy up repossessed property at, or very slightly below, market value as soon as it comes on the market. For example, during the recession of 1957–1958 a certain giant savings and loan on the West Coast, which we shall leave anonymous, had over 500 single-family residences in two tracts repossessed within a period of six months. This was in San Jose, which is about 50 miles south of San Francisco. In part, the repossessions came about because of temporary layoffs in aerospace and because the original builder could not sell all the homes he built. (Some of the repos were brand-new.) Rather than panic under the weight of so many houses (they were in the $15,000 price range with loans averaging $13,000 apiece, so that $6.5 million of the savings and loan's money was tied up), the savings and loan rented those homes that it could, opened a sales office, and proceeded to sell the others at full price. It took nearly three years, but eventually all were sold. Such is the condition of the repo market during a recession.

"FIXER-UPPERS"

However, because the opportunities to buy a repo at a reduced price do not exist in general, there is one area where it is possible to buy cheaply, and that is the area of "fixer-uppers." "Fixer-uppers," or "fixers," are usually homes which the former owner has left in a terrible state of disrepair when vacating. These present real headaches to lenders because without a major effort involving both labor and money, these houses cannot be sold on the open market (this type of repo is rarely any type of property other than a home). After all, who would buy a home with all the windows smashed out, half the doors torn from their hinges, holes in the walls both inside and out, built-in appliances stolen or demolished, toilets and sinks cracked, and walls smeared with filth? (Note: I have not exaggerated these conditions, but purposely understated them, though until you have seen a house that has been left in such a condition, this may be hard to believe. Often such destruction results not from the former owners, but from vandalism during the period after the owners leave and before the lender takes possession. In one house which I saw but did not buy, nearly 6 inches of manure had been laboriously hauled in, spread over the floors, and thrown on the walls.) The policy of most lenders who have conventional, or non-government-insured, loans on such houses is to fix them up and then sell. This costs money, but the lenders seem to feel that they lose less by paying for the cleanup, discounting the property, and selling for below market value. After all, how much below market would you have to lower the price before someone would buy the houses described above if they were not cleaned up?

GOVERNMENT REPOS

A unique condition exists in the area of government-insured loans. While the FHA and VA are not involved in many loans today, they did insure great numbers during the last two decades, and now many of these are coming up as repossessions. The process by which this works is quite simple. When the original borrower defaults, the loan company forecloses and then demands restitution from the FHA or VA for the money loaned. The government pays off and takes the house, hoping to resell it and get the money back.

In the past, both the FHA and VA have hired contractors to go in and completely refurbish these houses. They are painted inside and out, new appliances are installed to replace broken ones, windows are replaced and doors fixed. Then they are sold, in general for slightly *above* market value. The reasoning has been that the buyer is getting a completely redone home with a government-insured loan at usually lower than conventional interest rates, is paying no closing costs, and is putting very little down. The qualifying is similar to that for a new FHA or VA loan, except that for the VA, the buyer *does not have to be a veteran*. In general, the government's property management program has been successful. It is obvious that for the home buyer these houses represent a better than average deal. (Note: Should you be interested in purchasing such a home, you must do it through a broker—both the VA and FHA work almost exclusively through agents except in rural areas where no agents are available.)

The FHA

Very recently, the FHA has found that its inventory of such homes has exceeded its ability to refurbish and sell them. It began taking in more homes than it could get rid of. To offset this, it has begun selling homes at sometimes large discounts to investors.

The FHA discounts not only houses but bare land and small apartment buildings, usually of four or fewer units. They are often in poor condition, but if the investor is willing to fix them up, a profit can be made. As one FHA official said, "It's not worth our time, but to a small investor it could be a good deal." These sales are almost always advertised in local newspapers, or you can inquire by contacting any of the FHA regional offices listed in Table 7-1.

The sales are usually conducted as mail-bid auctions. Five or six properties will be lumped together for a single price in one "lot," or package. The FHA establishes a minimum bid, a figure below which it will not accept an offer. The minimum is arrived at after consideration is taken by the FHA on how much it has outstanding on the

Table 7-1

U.S. DEPARTMENT OF HOUSING AND URBAN DEVELOPMENT (FHA)

Main Office: 451 Seventh St. S.W.
                    Washington, D.C. 20410

Regional Offices:

Room 800
John F. Kennedy Federal Building
Boston, Massachusetts 02203

26 Federal Plaza
New York, New York 10007

Curtis Building
Sixth and Walnut Streets
Philadelphia, Pennsylvania 19106

Peachtree-Seventh Building
50 Seventh Street N.E.
Atlanta, Georgia 30323

300 South Wacker Drive
Chicago, Illinois 60606

Federal Building
819 Taylor Street
Fort Worth, Texas 76102

Federal Office Building
911 Walnut Street
Kansas City, Missouri 64106

Federal Building
1961 Stout Street
Denver, Colorado 80202

450 Golden Gate Avenue
Post Office Box 36003
San Francisco, California 94102

Arcade Plaza Building
1321 Second Avenue
Seattle, Washington 98101

---

properties and how much they are worth. A recent auction sale in Los Angeles, for example, involved five parcels. Each house had sustained some damage, but each was in an area of $25,000 or better homes. If all were in "doll-house" condition, it stood to reason that they should sell for a combined price of $125,000. The FHA was asking a minimum bid of $62,000.

At first glance, it might appear that a real profit could be made here. However, before you rush out to take advantage of the next FHA sale, at least the following cautions should be considered:

First, in each parcel the cost of fixing up has to be added to the purchase price. Even if the investor plans to do the work himself, he should add the cost of his labor (figured at so much an hour for as many hours as it takes) to the price. If the investor is unfamiliar with local building codes and requirements for fixing up property, he should consult a contractor who can inform him of requirements.

Second, the potential investor must consider the cost of resale. While the FHA usually pays all costs on its own sale, when it comes time for the investor to dispose of the homes, he will have to pay closing costs, which may include "stiff" points to help the next buyer get a loan as well as a broker's fee on each house (unless the investor has the time and ability to resell himself).

Finally, the potential investor has to consider the cash. The FHA normally takes back no loans on these homes. Anyone submitting a bid must normally include 5 to 10 percent of the offered price in the form of a cashier's check and present the balance in three weeks or less, in *cash*. This does not mean that the buyer needs to have all the cash himself. He can borrow it from a lending institution and then give it to the FHA. It does mean he has to have at least enough in cash to put down the 5 or 10 percent required with the deposit.

Financing on such purchases works as follows: When a purchaser has determined he is going to make an offer, he contacts the lending institution he has the best credit with, be it bank, savings and loan, mortgage banker, or private lender, and gets an appraisal and committment on each piece of property unless the deal is for a "blanket loan," one to cover all parcels. As part of the committment, the buyer must secure the lender's agreement to fund the money within the time limit imposed by the FHA. Finally, he must be prepared to supply either cash or secondary financing for the difference between the amount the lender will fund and the purchase price.

In the previous case of five properties with a minimum bid of $62,000, an investor consulted with me on a purchase. He was not willing to do any work himself, but I determined that it would take an average of $5,000 apiece to have the five properties refurbished. Added to this were a 6 percent commission and closing costs. On an average sales price of $25,000 a home, it all came to $7,500 for commissions and as much as another $7,500 for points and closing costs (figuring high to be safe). His expense sheet looked like this: FHA repo purchase:

Minimum bid	$ 62,000
Fixing up	25,000
Broker's commission on resale	7,500
Closing costs	7,500
	$102,000

Since the potential sales price on the homes was $125,000, he stood to make a $23,000 profit. Here is how much money he would have to invest. His best lender was a credit union of which he was a member. They were willing to loan 75 percent of the purchase price (presumably the minimum bid of $62,000), and they were willing to advance him another 75 percent of the $25,000 fixing-up cost at a later date and as the work was done.

$62,000	minimum bid
25,000	fixing up
$87,000	immediate costs
×0.75	
$65,250	loan amount
$21,750	cash required

The cash required was roughly $22,000. The closing costs and broker's costs would only be paid upon resale.

The investor pointed out that he stood to make $23,000 profit on a $22,000 investment. Since he expected to get the work done and the homes sold within a year, his rate of return on his investment would be over 100 percent.

I assured him that it was a magnificent investment if everything worked out right and *if* he could get the properties for $62,000. I pointed out that this was the *minimum bid*. It was possible to offer any amount higher.

Further, I pointed out that he should have added a certain amount for the risk involved. A house might burn down while he owned it (while insurance would cover the actual loss, it would not cover the future profit he was counting on), or future vandalism while the properties were unoccupied could raise the fixing-up costs, or a slump in the housing market could delay resale, perhaps for a long period of time.

He agreed and added 10 percent, or roughly $10,000, for risk. This cut his profit potential to about $13,000, still over 50 percent on the money to be invested. An excellent deal, I pointed out, *if* you can get the properties for $62,000. He considered, then decided to offer $65,000. His reasoning was that the $3,000 would offset other offers and still leave him a handsome profit.

The actual offer accepted by the FHA was well over $80,000 from another investor. When my associate came back with a look of amazement on his face and pointed out that just fixing-up and selling costs would more than eat up that figure, I pointed out that perhaps someone had figured differently.

If the buyer counted on selling *himself,* he could reduce the costs by eliminating broker's fees—$7,500 less. If the buyer did not figure the cost of his own work but nonetheless planned to do the labor, half the fixing up cost might be saved—$12,500. Add the two together and you arrive at $20,000. The buyer who was willing to do much of the work himself could offer $20,000 more than my associate. This immediately boosted the price into the $80,000 bracket. Even if my associate took no profit at all, he could not match this.

This story highlights one of the rules of repos—in order to make money on them, you have to plan to do much of the work yourself. If you do, chances are you can be like the final buyer. He stands to make *at least* $20,000 profit. Figuring a 10 percent, or $2,500, return on an investment of at least $25,000, he stands to make $17,500 for his year's labor. Not bad, if that is the kind of life you want.

COURT SALES

There are two other sources of repos or repo-like property, and these involve court sales. When an individual dies leaving property, often his or her heirs will sell the property during the probate period, or time when the estate is cleared. These sales are advertised in the newspaper and are handled, usually, through a lawyer. If you spend the time to examine notices in local papers and then estimate your costs quickly and submit them to the lawyer before others do, there is a good chance you can purchase a piece of property at a low enough price to make a profit. On probate, the property is often *not* in a run-down condition. However, since a purchase may take court approval, it is difficult to make one for considerably below market price. To get started in this field, simply check the paper in your area for probate sales. When one is listed, whom to contact will also be listed. This person will tell you if there is a minimum price and will usually provide a key so that you can inspect the premises. After that, it is up to your common sense.

The final area of repos involves buying foreclosed property *before* the loan company acquires title. The most common way of doing this also involves research. Before a piece of property can be taken back by a lender, a notice is very often advertised in a local paper of broad circulation. By scanning these notices it is possible to find out what loans are in default. Since it takes anywhere from 100 days to a year to actually transfer title, it is possible to approach either the person losing the property or the lender and buy it before, *for the loan amount*. When dealing with a lender, however, after a notice has been filed, this usually involves coming up with cash. (You may, of course, borrow much of the cash from another or even the same lender.) For example, if a lender has a $15,000 interest in a home which is in foreclosure, chances are that you as an investor will have to give the lender the full amount in order to remove the interest. Note, however, that if an investor attempts to pay off a lender before foreclosure is complete, the investor must get a deed from the original borrower (and presumably title insurance as well). Other-wise, the bizarre circumstance of an investor paying off another person's loan and having the other person still own the property could result

In actual practice this kind of purchase usually involves giving the departing owner a sum of money for signing the deed. Since, presumably, the property is going to be lost in any event, the money amounts to an unexpected bonus, and in many cases the owner is quite grateful.

The trick to this kind of purchase is to find a piece of property where the loan amount is far enough below the market value to make a purchase worthwhile, yet not so low that the property can be sold on the open market to anyone before foreclosure is completed. For example: If a home is worth $25,000 and it has a $10,000 loan on it which is being foreclosed upon because the current owner cannot keep up the payments, that owner would have no trouble in selling the house for, say, $22,000, paying off the loan and closing costs of $2,000, and pocketing the difference. However, if the loan were $21,000, such a sale might not be possible. An investor here might give the owner $500, assume the loan (or secure a new one), and obtain a $25,000 house for $3,500 below the market value. (Note: The $500 is a bonus the owner would not get if foreclosure were allowed to finish.)

In some rare cases, particularly with government loans, it is possible to get to the property soon enough to pick it up before the lender wants to be paid off. This is usually the case with people who have purchased with nothing down and are simply "walking away" from the home. Perhaps they have been transferred to another state by their employer, or for some reason they do not like the area, and do not have enough equity to make selling worthwhile. These may seem trivial reasons for abandoning a home, but there are a positively amazing number of such cases. For perhaps $50 or $100 the owners will be willing to sign over the deed. If the loan is only a month or so in arrears, it may be possible to make up back payments and continue on with the former loan. Including title investigation and insurance, a house conceivably can be bought for $200! It then usually becomes an excellent rental.

Working the repo market is a bit like what happens to stepchildren.

Although the cases cited were all relatively "clean" deals, often there is great emotional trauma involved with losing a home. Perhaps one spouse has died and the other cannot keep up the payments, or divorce or unemployment has broken up a family. In many cases events such as these are responsible for the existence of a repo. It is possible to work with repos and never see or get close to the human tragedy that swirls around them, particularly if you just deal with lenders. Here, the former owner is completely out of the picture and it is simply a business deal. But if you plan to delve deeply into the market, eventually you will come face to face with the grief of an individual losing his or her home. If you do not have the stomach for this, stay out. There are lots of other areas of real estate where you can make large profits.

8

Real Estate Tax Shelters and Tax Problems

Virtually anytime you make a profit or receive income, there is federal income tax to pay, and real estate is no exception. However, here certain tax advantages were built into the tax system largely to encourage building and development of residential property, and the advantages can often be utilized by the investor. This chapter provides insights into what taxes are applicable to real estate and how, primarily through the use of depreciation, these taxes can be deferred or postponed in order to shelter both income from real property and, on occasion, an individual's income from other sources. Note, however, that this chapter should not be construed as providing legal and tax advice. The investor reader should not rely on any legal or tax material in this book. All the programs described are imaginary and are presented solely to illustrate points being made. Because every individual's tax situation tends to be unique and because tax rulings are constantly changing, it is suggested that the reader who is an investor simply use this chapter as a guide to what sort of tax advantages and problems arise in real estate investments, and that he or she consult with their own financial planner, accountant, and attorney for legal and tax advice.

TAX ON GAIN

Anytime you sell a piece of property for more than you paid for it, you are going to be liable for a tax on the "gain," or profit. For example, if you bought a house for $20,000 and ten years later have sold it for $30,000, you are liable for taxes on the difference, or $10,000.

Residence Exclusion

An exclusion to the above rule applies if the property involved is your residence. The tax on the entire gain that you may have realized from the sale (or exchange) is postponed if the following two conditions are observed:

1. You buy and occupy another residence within one year either before or after the sale of your old personal residence (eighteen months after the sale if you build your new residence provided construction is started not more than one year after sale).

2. The *cost* of the new residence equals or exceeds the selling price of the old residence.

To apply the example of the property bought for $20,000 and sold for $30,000, say the property was your personal residence and if during the year before or after you sold you bought another residence which you occupied and paid at least $30,000, you have no income tax on your $10,000 gain to pay now. This does not mean that the tax is forgiven; it simply means that it is postponed until the time you sell your new residence. Let us say that after another ten years you sell the second piece of property for $40,000 and rent an apartment. If you do not buy another residence within a year for $40,000 or more, you now have a tax to pay. That tax is on the gain on your second house (bought for $30,000 sold for $40,000 equals $10,000) plus the gain on your first house which was postponed (bought for $20,000, sold for $30,000 equals $10,000), or a total of $20,000.

The tax on $20,000 would probably be a hefty sum; however, it could be postponed again simply by buying a new residence for the appropriate amount of money. There is no limit to the number of such postponements you can make, and many people never pay the tax, in the sense that they keep postponing it until they eventually get old and die.

Probably the most important advantage the individual can get from this law comes from the fact that you need not invest the funds made on the sale of your old property in your new residence. For example, in the sale we have been considering a $10,000 profit was made on the first residence. Not all of this has to be invested in the new home. Suppose a 90 percent loan were obtained on the $30,000 property, a $27,000 loan. Now only $3,000, or 10 percent down, need be invested. The remaining $7,000 of profit can be spent anywhere you want and for the moment is tax-free. Theoretically, if the individual could buy the second home for nothing down and the two conditions for postponement were met, the entire $10,000 could be used elsewhere and would not be immediately taxed.

It must be remembered, however, that when a sale is made and the money is not reinvested in a residence with the year limit, the tax will come due, and if the money has already been spent elsewhere, the individual could have to scramble to come up with the tax payment.

It should be noted that for simplicity our example just took into account sales price. In actual fact *adjusted* sales and purchase prices are taken into account. Adjusted sales price is usually the price after closing costs including broker's and mortgage fees have been paid and after the cost of any improvements and additions made to the property. In our previous example, if the owner's closing costs amounted to $3,000, even if he sold for $30,000, he would not show a $10,000 gain. Adjustments of $3,000 could be subtracted from his selling price, reducing his profit to $7,000. If during the period he owned the property he built a swimming pool at a cost of $7,000, this would be added to his tax base, raising it from $20,000 to $27,000. Both the pool and the closing costs would, in this example, negate his entire profit.

Also, it is not necessary to reinvest in a new residence of equal or higher value to receive *some* postponement. The two rules apply only if you want *all* the gain postponed. If, for example, the adjusted cost of the old residence were $30,000 and it sold for $40,000 and then a new residence of $35,000 value were purchased, the tax would normally only be due on the difference, or $5,000. The other $5,000 could be postponed.

Capital Gains

There is another method of reducing the tax paid on the gain realized from the sale of a piece of property, and it is called capital gains. The law on this came into effect to protect the capital that individuals were investing. It provides a definite advantage to anyone selling property for profit who cannot take advantage of the postponement because of residence just discussed.

If a piece of property is held over six months before it is sold, it qualifies as a long-term capital gain. Since most real estate investments are for long periods of time, most come under this rule. While an individual's income from his job, for example, is taxed at what is referred to as a regular rate, income derived from the sale of property held over six months is taxed at a special capital gains rate.

Briefly there are two methods of computing the tax. The first is to take the total gain, divide it in half, and tack this amount onto an individual's regular income. For those who are in less than a 25 percent tax bracket, this is the most advantageous course. For those in a higher tax bracket there is an *alternate method*. It is simply to pay a flat tax rate computed as 25 percent of the first $50,000 and about 35 percent of the balance. Both methods, since they permit paying a much lower amount than the regular rate, provide an advantage for the investor who can claim them.

As an example, let us consider the case of Mr. Jones, who buys a duplex for $30,000 and six years later sells for $40,000. For the moment we shall not consider depreciation (to be discussed shortly), but shall assume that at the time he sold he showed a gain of $10,000. Under regular tax this amount would be added to his regular income, which we will arbitrarily say was $15,000 in salary from his job as an insurance salesman, for a total of $25,000.

However, since the $10,000 came from the sale of a capital asset, real estate, it can be declared as capital gains. Since Mr. Jones is in a fairly low tax bracket (under 25 percent), he simply ignores one-half of his gain and adds the other half, $5,000, to his regular income, for a total of $20,000. It is easy to see that the income tax one has to pay on $20,000 is going to be less than that on $25,000.

The alternate method mentioned above that can be used for figuring capital gains is particularly useful for those who happen to be in the above-50 percent tax bracket. Consider the case of Mr. Reed, who makes considerably over $50,000 a year and is in the 50 percent tax bracket. Let us say that, instead of a duplex, he sells an apartment building and the profit at the time of sale is $60,000. If the $60,000 were simply cut in half and $30,000 were added to Mr. Reed's regular income, he would end up paying tax on a total of $80,000 ($50,000 regular income plus one-half of the profit, or $30,000). This would put him close to the 70 percent tax bracket, assuming he is single and does not have other deductions. He would be paying 70 percent on his whole income including the $30,000 profit. The alternate method would be to his advantage. He simply takes 25 percent of the first $50,000 and pays that in tax (that is equivalent to paying a 50 percent tax on half the capital gain). He then takes the $10,000 left from his $60,000 profit and cuts it in half (treating it like normal capital gain) and adds one-half to his regular income, increasing it from $50,000 to

$55,000. He now pays a little over 50 percent tax on this amount. It is easy to see that with the alternate method, Mr. Reed avoids paying a 70 percent tax and ends up paying a little over 50 percent on his taxable profit. The savings in Mr. Reed's tax bracket could be as much as 20 percent of $30,000, or $6,000.

Advantages for the Elderly   If you are over sixty-five at the time you sell your home, the government allows a special "once in a lifetime" tax savings for you, provided you meet certain requirements. These are that you lived in the property for five out of the last eight years, ending on the date of the sale; that the property was your residence; and that you are not reinvesting your profit (in which case the tax might be deferred). The savings, called an "exclusion for the elderly," work in the following manner:

If the house is sold for up to, but not more than, $20,000, the entire profit is forgiven. If the house is sold for over $20,000, a moderately complicated formula is used to figure the taxable profit. It is the fraction which $20,000 is of the adjusted sales price. An example will explain how this works. Assume the sales price of a house owned by someone who qualifies for this exclusion is $50,000 and the base is $10,000. When we subtract the $10,000, we arrive at a profit of $40,000. What percent of this profit is taxed and what percent forgiven? The formula specifies that we have to arrive at that fraction which $20,000 is of the sales price—$20,000/$50,000, or $2/5$. We now simply multiply $2/5$ by the profit of $40,000 and we discover that the amount to be forgiven is $2/5 \times \$40,000 = \$16,000$. Our elderly couple now pay capital gains on the balance of the $40,000, or $24,000. A considerable savings for them.

Problems of a Dealer in Real Estate   A word of caution must be inserted here regarding the individual who buys and sells a large number of properties. The various tax advantages are designed for individuals who have other income and, so to speak, dabble in real estate on the side. If, however, one's sole income comes from the buying and selling of real estate, for tax purposes this individual may be declared a dealer in real estate, and he will not be able to claim the capital gains advantage. The general rule is vague, but usually, anyone who buys and sells more than four or five pieces of property a year (as owner, not agent) may be classified as a dealer.

TAX SHELTERS

Thus far we have been concerned with tax areas involved with the sale of real estate. There is another entire area that deals with tax advantages one can obtain while owning property. These are dubbed *tax shelters*. The term refers to the various ways one can get out of the rain of income taxes that is constantly pouring down.

In general tax shelters work because an owner of property, particularly income-producing residential property such as an apartment building, is allowed to deduct certain items from his income which often appear much larger on paper than the income itself. Because of this the income itself is not taxed, and the surplus "loss" can be applied to other regular income. Let us take an example.

Mr. Gray buys a $200,000 apartment building. After expenses he shows a profit of $12,000 a year. But his paper, or "accounting," deductions show a loss after those expenses of $18,000 a year. Since tax is only paid on profit, Mr. Gray deducts $12,000 from $18,000 and shows a $6,000 paper loss. Now he does not have to pay any tax on the $12,000 actual income. It is tax-free. In addition, he may apply the difference between the accounting loss and the actual income ($6,000) to income from another source. If Mr. Gray also made $15,000 a year in his job as a fireman, this income could be reduced by the $6,000 to just $9,000.

That $6,000 applied to reduce other income is called a tax shelter. In Mr. Gray's case it will probably be worth only $700 in cash that he will not have to pay in tax he otherwise would have owed, because he is in a low tax bracket. However, if Mr. Gray were in a 50 percent tax bracket or higher (making $60,000 a year), that $6,000 would be worth half, or $3,000, in actual cash saved that otherwise would have gone to the government in taxes. It is easy to see why as our income increases, we become more and more interested in tax shelters.

Depreciation

The biggest source of a tax shelter is depreciation. *Depreciation* means simply loss in value. As it is applied to real estate, it means loss in value due to time and use. Land can never be depreciated, because theoretically it never loses its usage (although the minerals in land can be used up—this is called *depletion* and is a considerable tax advantage with regard to oil and gas). What is depreciated in real estate, then, is the building on the land.

If the building on the land is used for pleasure, as is a home residence, it cannot be depreciated because the owner, presumably, receives pleasure from the building for its life-span. If, however, an individual invests money in a building, such as an apartment house, it can be depreciated because, presumably, as the building grows older its value diminishes and the amount of money he *invests* is lost. For example, say you build an apartment building for $100,000 cash and it brings in a monthly return on your investment for thirty years, at which time it is too old to be rented and must be torn down for scrap. At the end of thirty years your investment capital is gone (disregarding the income produced, which is just a return on capital). The government allows the owner of such a building to write off a certain portion of his loss against his taxes each of the thirty years he owns the building.

As mentioned earlier, a government survey indicates that the life expectancy of an average apartment building is between fifty and seventy-five years; practically speaking, however, the longest time any such building is depreciated on paper is normally forty years. This provides a boon to the owner in the sense that he is depreciating the building *faster* than its physical loss of value. In addition, the government in many cases allows an *accelerated* depreciation of up to 200 percent to the owner. And finally, each new owner can start depreciating the property all over again (although with limitations on accelerated depreciation).

The net result is that the difference between the paper loss and the actual loss of value can be large, providing a tremendous tax advantage for those able to use it. (And with the inflation rampant during a modern recession, apartment buildings do not decline in value at all, provided they are reasonably maintained.)

It should be noted, however, that the government has taken steps to limit these artificial accounting losses. New regulations may limit the loss to just the particular property or another piece of property of like kind. Such rules have been drafted, but have not been implemented as of this writing.

Methods of Depreciating Buildings There are basically three methods. The first is called *straight line*. This is the simplest and by far the easiest to understand. It means, basically, that the same amount is depreciated each year of the life of the building. If the lifespan is determined to be twenty years, then one-twentieth is depreciated each year. At the end of twenty years, the entire value has been depreciated. If we plot a graph of the twenty-year period we will see that the decline is a straight line (See Figure 4).

Another method is *declining balance*. It is a bit more sophisticated but not really any harder to understand. A declining balance is used

FIGURE 4 Straight-line Method of Depreciation

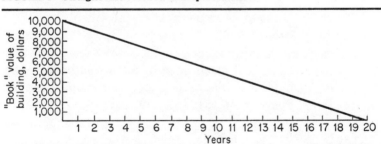

NOTE: In the case of a $10,000 building, the depreciated value drops by exactly $500 each year if the life of the building is 20 years.

only when the depreciation is accelerated, that is, when it is above 100 percent. It is easy to see that if, for example, we were depreciating a new apartment building at 200 percent for forty years and used the straight-line method, at the end of the forty-year period we would have, in fact, depreciated twice its value. However appealing this may be, it is something the government understandably does not allow. To depreciate a building at 200 percent or 150 percent or 125 percent, we simply take the percentage we are using and apply it to the remaining value of the building each year. For example, if we have a $100,000 new building we are depreciating for forty years at 200 percent by the declining-balance method, our first year's write-off would be $100,000 divided by 40, or $2,500, which we would multiply by 200 (our rate of depreciation), yielding $5,000:

$$\$100,000 \div 40 = \$2,500$$
$$\underline{\times\ 200\%}$$
$$\$5,000 \text{ (first-year depreciation)}$$

The next year we do the same thing, but instead of figuring the value of our building at $100,000, we now use a value of $95,000. We subtract the depreciation we have already allowed. Our figures would look like this:

$$\$95,000 \div 40 = \$2,375$$
$$\underline{\times\ 200\%}$$
$$\$4,750 \text{ (second year's depreciation)}$$

As you can see, the depreciation on the second year is less than that for the first year, but much more than it would be under the straight-line method. It declines even more for the third year. We subtract $4,750 from $95,000 to get $90,250, and

$$\$90,250 \div 40 = \$2,256.25$$
$$\underline{\times\ 200\%}$$
$$\$4,512.50 \text{ (third year's depreciation)}$$

Each year the amount depreciated is less as the balance declines. Under this method the greatest amount of depreciation is taken in the first few years with very small depreciation in the latter years. This method is particularly useful for someone with an outside income that needs sheltering. It must be remembered, however, that the shelter only works well in the early years when there is a large depreciation.

There is one final method called *sum of the years' digits*, but it is currently allowed only on the 200 percent rate of depreciation. It simply involves adding up the number of years to be depreciated and then dividing each year by the total. For example, if the useful life were determined to be five years, the sum of five years would be added: $1 + 2 + 3 + 4 + 5 = 15$. The first year five-fifteenths would be depreciated, the second year four-fifteenths, the third year three-fifteenths, and so on.

Depreciation on Different Types of Property   It is possible to depreciate any income property using the straight-line method. However, because accelerated depreciation can provide tax shelters, it is important to know the maximum allowable depreciation on various types of buildings.

RESIDENTIAL INCOME PROPERTY RENTALS: A piece of property normally qualifies as residential if 80 percent or more of its income comes from rentals.

1. *New residential income* may normally be depreciated at 200 percent using either the sum of the years' digits or the declining balance. However, for apartment buildings the term is usually forty years (forty-five years for a house).

2. *Used residential income* may be depreciated at a rate of 125 percent using the declining-balance method. The term may often be as short as twenty years.

3. *Trailer parks* can only be depreciated using the straight-line method; however, the term can be as short as twelve years.

COMMERCIAL BUILDINGS: Commercial buildings can be depreciated at a rate of 150 percent if they are new. The term is forty to fifty years. Used nonresidential buildings must use the straight-line method.

"REHABS": Certain low-income rental housing rehabilitated under the Department of Housing and Urban Development (HUD-FHA) may be depreciated using the straight-line method over the incredibly short term of just five years. The great advantage of depreciation is that it initially reduces taxes. There are, however, disadvantages, which will be dealt with extensively later in this chapter under the heading "Tax Problems."

Prepaid Interest

In addition to depreciation, it is possible to get a first year of owner-ship tax advantage by prepaying interest on the mortgages on a piece of property. This may be of particular use if the owner has a sizable income in one year that he wants to shelter. The government nor-mally allows an investor to prepay all the interest for the remainder of the year in which he purchases his investment, plus one additional year. If, for example, you purchase an apartment building on April 1, you can prepay the interest for the remaining nine months of that year, plus the next year. It must be remembered, however, that in order to claim this type of deduction the interest must in fact be paid. It is only useful if the investor has a lot of cash to use that would otherwise go to Uncle Sam. However, prepaying interest has draw-backs.

There are basically two difficulties with prepaid interest. The first is that after the first year you have to continue prepaying your interest in order to get a write-off. In other words, the second year you have to prepay the third year's interest; the third, the fourth year's interest; and so on. In any year that you do not prepay, the income from the property could conceivably be larger than your other deductions and would then become taxable gain.

The second difficulty with prepaid interest comes at the time of sale. If you have been prepaying and you subsequently sell your property, for example, on July 1, you will discover that you have already paid interest on your mortgages from July 1 until December 31. However, you will not own the property during that period. The mortgagees will send back the six months prepaid interest and it will come to you as regular income on which you will have to pay regular taxes.

Other Costs Which May Be Written Off

Normally, all the necessary costs associated with the operation of income-producing property may be deducted from income on a one-for-one basis. For example, if you spend $100 in advertising, you can deduct $100 from income. The same holds true with repairs, upkeep, maintenance, management, and so on. But one word of caution must be said with regard to fixing up. In general, if an investor spends more than 5 percent of the total value of the building in fixing up, this could be construed as improving the property rather than repairing it. Major improvements may have to be written off over the entire life of the building, rather than just the year in which they are made.

For more detailed examples of how tax sheltering works with regard to individual ownership, see Chapter 2, where Howard and Gail VanTill purchase and sell various items for profit yet shield their profits. For an example of how tax sheltering works for a group such as a limited-partnership syndication, see Chapter 6, where a comprehensive example is given.

TAX PROBLEMS

Thus far we have been concerned with how to shelter income and how to reduce the tax on profit at the time of sale. There is one final area that should be covered—problems that can arise in dealing with taxation on real estate.

Recapture of Depreciation

Depreciation, unfortunately, can be a two-edged sword. While providing a shelter when we own a piece of property, it can come back and hit us with an enormous profit when we sell. The problem can be divided into two areas. The first is *declining basis*.

A declining tax basis occurs whenever a piece of property is depreciated. It is most easily understood in the form of an example. Suppose that we purchase a piece of property for $1.4 million and that the value of the building is $1 million even. Further, let us assume we depreciate it using the straight-line method for twenty years. After ten years we have depreciated half the value, or $0.5 million. Now we decide to sell, and for some reason (perhaps we have not maintained the building or the area has deteriorated) we sell for no profit but for exactly what we paid, $1.4 million. We broke even, right? Wrong! We show a $0.5 million tax profit.

As the building is depreciated, its tax basis goes down. We started with a $1 million building, but after ten years our building has a tax basis of only $500,000 (the other $500,000 having been depreciated). If we sell for more than $500,000, we show a tax profit. In order to actually break even from a tax standpoint, we would need to sell for no more than $900,000 total (the cost of the land plus the tax base). Since we sold for $1.4 million, we show a $0.5 million profit on which we have to pay income tax.

This may not be as bad as it seems after some thought. First let us figure our tax. Since we held the building for more than six months, it is deemed a long-term capital investment and we are taxed only on the basis of capital gains—25 percent of the first $50,000 plus 35 percent of the balance. Our tax on the half-million-dollar accounting, or paper, profit is $170,000. For ten years, however, we presumably have been paying off a mortgage. Assuming ours was a 75 percent loan, or a little over $1 million on our $1.4 million purchase price, chances are we have paid down more than $160,000 on our principal. (The actual amount would depend on the term of the loan and the interest rate.) Consequently when we sell, we will probably have enough money coming out of the mortgage reduction to pay the taxes, although we may not show any profit in cash in our hands. If the building is held long enough and not overly financed, the investor usually comes out all right.

But now consider the same case if we had elected to depreciate the building by the accelerated method at 125 percent (assuming it was a used building). Now, at the end of ten years, our tax basis is down to roughly $400,000, $100,000 of which the accelerated method is responsible for. When we now decide to sell, our profit is $600,000. We can declare $500,000 of it as a capital gain, and we pay the same tax of roughly $170,000 as above. However, most of the profit caused by *accelerating* the depreciation (the $100,000) we *cannot* claim as capital gains. It must be figured as *regular income*. This is called *recapture of depreciation*.

Recapture of depreciation occurrs whenever one has used an accelerated method of depreciation and then sells for above the tax base. In this case the $100,000 of income caused by recapture would be taxed in the regular way. If the investor is a married individual with normal deductions, the regular tax on $100,000 is roughly $45,000. (The advantages of capital gains can clearly be seen here—$45,000 tax on $100,000 of regular income, but only $160,000 tax on $500,000 of capital gains income.)

Our situation is not quite as desperate as it may at first seem, however, for there is one item on our side. The government forgives the regular tax on the recapture of depreciation if we hold the property long enough. The rule is that you have to hold the investment for 100 months. For every month thereafter, 1 percent is forgiven. Since we sold after ten years, or 120 months, 20 percent of the $100,000 goes from the regular income side to the capital gains side. (If we held for 200 months, or 16.7 years, all the accelerated amount would be considered capital gains.)

We still have to pay regular tax on $80,000, but we may hope that the decline in our mortgage will still be enough to cover us.

Foreclosure

The case is not quite so cheery for the individual or syndicate that loses a building through foreclosure. Let us take the case of the syndicate that buys a building purely for its tax-sheltering advantage. Say the building and land again cost $1.4 million, divided the same as above ($1 million for the building, the rest for the land). Instead of putting down one-fourth, however, the investors get second- and third-mortgage interest-only loans. (Remember, they can deduct all interest, and they are interested only in the shelter aspect.) The mortgages total $1.35 million. The investment might look like this:

First $1 million	payable interest only at 9% for twenty years—balloon payment at end—$90,000 a year
Second $0.2 million	payable interest only at 10% for ten years—balloon payment at end—$20,000 a year
Third $0.15 million	payable interest only at 12% for five years—balloon payment at end—$18,000 a year

The annual interest payment is $128,000. Let us assume the syndicate depreciates the building at 125 percent for twenty years, or a total of roughly $185,000 for the first three years. Further, let us assume that all other expenses total $32,000 a year and that the income from the building is $150,000 per year.

Interest	$128,000
All other expenses	32,000
	$150,000 total expenses
	$150,000 total income

As we can see, the depreciation of more than $150,000 is all an accounting loss *over and above* the other expenses. Under current tax laws this can be applied to an individual's other *regular* income. If the investors are in the 50 percent tax bracket, the $185,000 plus means a savings to them in actual dollars of $92,500. By simply holding the building and paying interest, they have made back their initial $50,-

000 plus a profit of $42,500—all through tax sheltering. A "sweet deal"?

The number of investors over the past years who have thought so in incredible. It is not a sweet deal at all—it is a bad deal because it is *leveraged* out of all proportion. Anytime you have to borrow more than 75 to 80 percent to buy an *income* investment (this does not apply to homes), you are overleveraged and asking for foreclosure. The slightest increase in vacancies can wipe you out.

Let us assume that this is what happens in our example after three years. The loans foreclose, but since they were all purchase-money mortgages and the building and land were the entire collateral, the investors walk away scot-free with the profit they have already made by sheltering, right? Not so. They have tax to pay!

Remember, depreciation lowers the tax base. In this case it is lowered by the $185,000 depreciated. Since the loans foreclose at full value (remember, they were interest-only mortgages designed to provide the highest tax-shelter advantage), the amount the property is taken back for is the loan amount—$1.35 million (the syndicate's original $50,000 capital is of course wiped out). This becomes the *selling* base for tax purposes. But the tax base is much lower, $185,000 lower than the original price. The tax base is $1,215,000, for a difference of $135,000 from the selling base. This is a real gain or profit as far as the government is concerned, and now the investors have to pay taxes on this amount. Even if it all were capital gains, it would just about wipe out the $42,500 profit shown after three years from sheltering. (It would actually reduce this profit over investment to just $250.) But an accelerated depreciation was used, and some of the gain will face regular tax. This will not only eliminate all the profit but cause a loss on the investors' original $50,000. They would have been far better off to just put the money in a bank.

The moral of this story is that you should always consider the economic realities before you invest. In real estate it is possible to pay taxes on a loss.

OTHER "LOOPHOLES" YOU
SHOULD KNOW ABOUT

Tax-free Exchange

It is possible to postpone the payment of taxes on the sale of income property if you trade for a like piece of property of equal value. For a complete illustration see the discussion of Howard and Gail VanTill's purchase of Mr. Thomas's apartment building and trailer park in Chapter 2.

"29 Percent Downers"

Normally the government requires you to pay taxes in the year of sale on the full amount of profit. There is one exception, however, which relates to amortization.

If you sell a piece of property and the buyer will purchase it in at least two or more payments, you need only report the profit *as you receive it* This is of particular advantage to individuals who either own a piece of property free and clear or hold a large equity in it. This regulation, however, is subject to a condition, and that is that with regard to real estate, *the amount of money collected in the year of sale may not exceed 30 percent*. It has become common practice for those who have large equities in property to request "only 29 percent down." This is as close to 30 percent as possible. The tax on 29 percent of the selling price is bound to be in a lower bracket than the tax on 100 percent of the selling price.

9

Eleven Great Investment Opportunities

It had been said often enough to be true that every time there is a war, the nations fighting use the armaments, strategies, and goals of the previous war. The point is that nations have great difficulty keeping up with changing times. Individuals are much the same way, particularly when it comes to investments. Because in the past so much money was made in bare land sales in the Western states and in those portions of the Eastern states away from the cities, people today still often think of bare land first when considering real estate investment. Yet, with certain exceptions, many investors in bare land today lose their shirts.

Next in line in interest of novice investors are condominiums. Great stories are told of the advertising man in New York who bought a condominium (apartment—not the whole building) in Queens for $35,000 and two years later sold it for $60,000—or the TV producer in Phoenix who made $15,000 profit in just three months by buying into a condominium just as it was completed. Such tales are probably true, of early 1973 and 1972 and possibly even 1971. But I doubt that you have heard one such tale recently. One leading nationwide mortgage banking company stopped making any loans for new condominiums in mid-1973 because of the glut on the market. It was widely reported in the news media that the Beverly Hills Bank Corporation, which included in its assets the Beverly Hills Bank and a savings and loan institution, was forced into *receivership* in early 1974, reportedly because of excessive loans in the condominium field. "Condos" are no longer the great investment they once were.

In order to keep abreast of what are really good real estate investments I like to refer to the chart presented here as Table 9-1. It lists most real estate investments as well as a good number of investments in other areas and compares them in the context of today's economy in terms of profit potential, risk, tax shelter, and leverage. (Leverage is the amount of your money you have to invest as compared with the amount of money you control. If you invest $1,000 and control $20,000 you have high leverage. If you invest $1,000 and control $1,000 you have low leverage.) A detailed explanation of each type of investment follows.

TRAILER PARKS

I rate these as one of the best real estate investments. The profit potential is great; the risk, if the purchase is properly financed, is almost nonexistent; and the leverage is fairly good. In addition—and this is the biggest advantage—there are few people yet aware of the potential here.

Trailer parks have been around virtually as long as there have been cars. Trailers were advertised as early as 1912, and by 1920 "yachts of the road," which were really motorized homes, were being advertised in leading publications for $700 to $800. Buyers had to have a place to park these and the trailer park was born.

These increased in numbers gradually over the years, but saw a great boom after World War II. During the late forties and early fifties

Table 9-1. Eleven Great Investments for Today

These investments are graded according to four criteria: First, what is their potential for yielding a relatively short-term *profit* (under five years)? Second, how great is the *risk* involved to the average investor? Third, what is the typical *leverage* obtainable? (Do you have to invest a lot or a little to control the property?) Fourth, is the *tax shelter* offered large or small? Investments other than real estate are also listed for comparison, with an explanation at the end of the chapter.

	Profit	Risk	Leverage	Shelter
Trailer parks	High	Low	Moderate	Moderate
Moderate-income apartments	Low	Low	Moderate	High
Medium-income apartments (older units)	High	Low	Moderate–High	High
High-rent apartments	High	Moderate	Low–Moderate	Moderate-High
Condominiums	Moderate	Moderate	High	Low
Houses	High	Low	High	Low
Duplexes	Low	Low	High	Moderate
Vacation homes	Low-High	Moderate	Moderate	None
Bare land (large sections)	High	High	Low	None
Bare land (small lots)	Low	High	High	None
Conversions	High	High	Moderate–High	Moderate
Non-real estate investments:				
Stocks	Low	High	Low	None
Commodities	High	High	High	None
Gold and silver	High	High	Low	None
Coins and paintings	High	Moderate	Low	None
Novelties	Moderate	High	Low	None

literally thousands of trailer parks were built across the country. Many of these had facilities for only thirty to fifty trailers but were considered adequate in their day, for demand was not yet high. Housing costs in those years were still fairly low, and there were few people who chose the alternative of a trailer park as a permanent residence.

Today the story is different. We are in a modern recession, and its ramifications are everywhere. Our chronic high rate of inflation has been a catastrophe for people on fixed incomes. There are an estimated 20 million Americans, according to Department of Labor statistics, who depend on social security for either their entire income or the major portion of it. Even with the recent increases, the amount a retired family of two has to spend each month for all living expenses can be under $300. The Federal Housing Administration uses a rule of thumb to determine how much of a person's total monthly income should go for housing expense. It estimates that *no more* than one-fourth can safely be spent for housing. That means a couple with a $300 a month income (and admittedly this is high for the majority of retirees on pension) can only spend $75 per month for shelter. Where can anyone find housing that is in a decent neighborhood and that is clean, modern, and aesthetically acceptable for that figure?

Many pensioners faced with having to pay two or three times the $75 figure have eaten into their life savings to upgrade their housing. This is a self-limiting proposition, for once these savings, usually fairly moderate, are gone, their standard of living is sure to drop. Others have found a solution. For a one-time expenditure of anywhere from $2,000 to $15,000 they have bought a mobile home and have had it placed in a modern trailer park. Here they can live on $75 a month or less total monthly rental expense.

In response to the chronic high inflation rate the demand for modern trailer parks has quadrupled. Investors, sensing the demand, have poured great amounts of capital into *new* trailer parks. However, many have had sizable losses. Here is why.

Today's modern trailer park, if recently built, will likely have a swimming pool, a clubhouse, even a small restaurant and perhaps a grocery store. In addition it will probably have accommodations for 100 or more trailers. To build a trailer park in the 1940s or 1950s required a minimum amount of capital. Virtually all that was required was the grading and asphalting of a network of roads, the pouring of concrete for trailer pads, and the distribution of utility outlets at the pads. Land costs were then still fairly low. An entire trailer-park setup could cost anywhere from $15,000 to $25,000.

Today the story is different. Land costs have skyrocketed everywhere, and construction costs have kept pace. In addition, today's clientele at a first-rate trailer park expects extensive landscaping, a clubhouse, a swimming pool, etc. The cost today of constructing a modern park can be anywhere from $3,000 to $7,000 per pad, depending on how elaborate it is. This means that a park of 100 trailers at even the lower figure could cost $300,000.

Nonetheless, the profit potential still remains. A modern pad can rent for anywhere from $50 to $100 dollars a month. At the lower figure, assuming complete occupancy, the monthly return is $5,000 and the yearly return $60,000 gross on a $300,000 investment. Of course there are maintenance costs, loan-retirement costs, utility bills, etc., but the potential for profit can be clearly seen.

What has hurt many investors who have attempted to build new trailer parks is *the time it takes to get complete occupancy.* Some few lucky parks are built in such a prime location that occupants swarm in even before the park is completed, but these tend to be unusual deals where a choice piece of land for one reason or another was made available at below-market cost. Remember, a trailer park, unlike any other kind of real estate development, is totally *horizontal.* Even in a single-story apartment building a fairly large number of units can be clustered together on a small piece of ground. In trailer parks, the amount of land occupied is enormous, for what is being rented out is basically the land space itself. The need for large parcels of land to accommodate trailer parks has forced builders to move their developments to the outskirts of metropolitan areas where land values are lower. This reduces the cost of the park but has an inherent weakness. Pensioners, many of whom no longer drive, are hesitant to move any significant distance away from metropolitan areas with their shopping and recreational conveniences.

The developer who builds a new trailer park at the far edge of the city, even if it is a high-quality park, may have to wait six months to two years before he gets total occupancy, *if he ever does*

Consequently, real estate investors who have built a $300,000 trailer park and who have had loans of $250,000 with large monthly payments, taxes, and utilities and maintenance costs have in many cases "gone belly up." The foreclosure rate on new trailer parks is surprisingly high, and not surprisingly, lending institutions are tending to shy away from lending money on such projects.

But I have not led you all this way only to conclude that trailer parks are not really a good investment; take comfort, for the best is yet to come.

Remember all those small trailer parks that were built during the ten-year period after World War II, tens of thousands of them all across the country? Well, they are still around, and therein lies the great profit potential for both the large and small investor.

These "Ma and Pa" trailer parks with their thirty or so pads were built at the outskirts of the cities twenty years ago. But since then the cities have grown, and now they are quite often in very desirable locations. In addition, over the course of years the vast majority of owners of these parks have paid off whatever mortgages they had on them and now own them free and clear. And in many cases current owners *are willing to take back the financing themselves*. This means that the buyer does not have to go to a lending institution for a loan. And last and most significant, in an overwhelming majority of older trailer parks that I have seen, improvements have not been made over the years—utility outlets are often in disrepair, pads are cracked or, worse, disintegrated, roads are not paved, and landscaping has been totally neglected—yet these same parks invariably *have total occupancy*. The reason, of course, is simple. The rents have not been raised. It is not uncommon to find a tenant still paying $25 to $30 a month for a trailer pad in such a park.

Like apartment buildings, the price of a trailer park is often found by means of a "cost factor." While houses have their prices determined by a comparison of what similar houses have sold for in the past, income-producing property has its price determined most often by the amount of income it can produce. The cost factor is an arbitrary figure that is used to give a price based on the amount of income. It is sometimes called a "multiplier." The cost factor is arrived at by use of a complex equation that takes into account the cost of reproducing the property, a comparison of what other similar properties have sold for in relation to their incomes, and the general health of the economy. Suffice to say that the cost factor for trailer parks, like that for apartments, is anywhere between 5 and 7.

(Note: As just described, the income multiplier applies only to yearly *gross* income. Some feel an alternate method works better. This is to use a "net income multiplier." This usually works in the following manner: All the monthly income on a piece of property is added up, then the normal expenses—operating costs, maintenance, etc.—are subtracted. This leaves a "net monthly income," which is now multiplied by a different group of arbitrary numbers. These range from 100 to 120 and give another estimate of the building's value. The exact number chosen, like the 5 through 7 in our example, tends to depend on how the person making the decision feels, with higher numbers assigned for more desirable property and lower numbers for less desirable pieces.)

If a trailer park is renting its pads for $25 per month and has thirty pads, it is bringing in $750 a month, or $9,000 a year, assuming full occupancy. If it is the old run-down sort of trailer park we are talking about, we would use the smaller cost factor of 5 (reserving the higher figure of 7 for modern, newer parks) and arrive at a price of $45,000. While this may seem arbitrary, it is in fact an extremely useful and highly accurate method of arriving at price on income-producing residential property.

The individual who would buy a $45,000 trailer park would undoubtedly need at least 25 percent of the purchase price, or $11,250, to make the deal. While this may be too high a figure for the beginning investor, it is possible to make the same deal with ten friends each putting up $1,125. For details on how to accomplish this see Chapter 6 on syndication.

The advantages of buying an older trailer park can best be seen by taking an actual case.

Marsh Green sold the home he had lived in for eighteen years and after paying taxes suddenly found he had $21,000 to invest. (See Chapter 8 on taxes for ways to avoid paying high taxes on the sale of your home.) His children had grown up and married, and he and his wife wanted something they could work at, a little business, in addition to his regular job as a postal clerk. After careful consideration he decided to buy the Sleepy Hollow trailer court. It was twenty years old and beaten up, but in a fairly good section of Denver. The owner had advertised the park for sale in the *Denver Post,* and to Marsh Green it seemed like a good deal. The owner wanted $45,000 and was willing to accept 29 percent down in cash and carry the balance himself.

The reason the owner specified 29 percent down is based on the tax laws. Obviously he owned the trailer court free and clear. As already noted, federal tax laws are so written that if he received more than 30 percent in cash, he would have to declare the entire purchase price as income in the year he sold and pay tax on the cash received. If he received 30 percent or less as a down payment, he would have to declare only the down payment as income in the year he received it and could spread out the balance over the years that he actually was to get it in income. Sellers often specify 29 percent down instead of the full 30 so as to insure against any error that might occur in escrow that would give them a slightly higher down payment and negate their tax advantage.

Marsh had to put up $13,050 in cash on the Sleepy Hollow trailer park, and the seller was willing to take back a first loan for twenty years at 8 percent interest for a balance of $31,950.

The deal was handled through a Realtor who took care of all escrow problems, with the seller paying the commission. It looked like this for Marsh:

Price	$45,000
Down	$13,050
Loan	$31,950

The trailer park was in fact the $45,000 park described earlier. It had 30 pads fully rented at $25 a month, bringing in $9,000 a year. A cost factor of 5 gave it its reasonable price.

Marsh bought a house trailer of his own and, after asking around among the tenants, found one who was planning to leave soon, got the tenant to agree to leave earlier, and moved his own trailer onto the pad. He had spent roughly $13,000 in buying the trailer court (including closing costs) and put $2,000 down on his own trailer, which now left him $6,000 of his original starting capital of $21,000 to use in rehabilitating the park.

At this time his income and expense statement looked like this:

INCOME	$8,700 annually (twenty-nine pads at $25 apiece—remember he was using one himself)
EXPENSES	
First loan	$4,800 at $400 per month
Taxes	$1,800 annually (these are normally quite low for trailer parks because basically there is only land to tax)
Maintenance	$1,200 (he handled most of this himself)
Utilities	Paid for by each tenant
Total	$7,800

His profit was $900 a year—roughly 5 percent a year on the $21,000 he had to invest, not a handsome return when you figure inflation at anywhere from 8 to 11 percent. However, Marsh was an enterprising individual with a good head on his shoulders. He still had $6,000 of his original capital. This he used to asphalt the roads and pour concrete on some of the most decayed pads. With the very few dollars that remained he bought shrubbery, and he himself planted, pulled weeds, and in general did a fine job of landscaping the court. Of course it was not a professional job, and he had no swimming pool or recreation house, but the place looked better than it had in years; all the tenants agreed this was the case when he asked them. Then, he went on to tell them, they should not mind it when he raised the rents $10 per pad. The rent had not been raised for nearly seven years, he had learned from the previous owner, and with inflation the way it was he simply had to keep pace, he told the renters.

Two moved out; seven were outraged and complained bitterly, but agreed that even $35 a month was not high. The rest paid without complaint. The two vacancies were quickly filled.

Marsh's profit and loss statement was greatly improved. Without increasing expenses, he had increased his income by $290 per month, or $3,480 a year, to a total of $4,380 a year, roughly a 20 percent a year return on his $21,000 investment.

What was even more dramatic in the way of profit potential was that by raising rents, Marsh immediately raised the value of his trailer park. Remember, pricing is done on the basis of income. Assuming the same cost factor of 5 times the gross income (formerly $9,000 a year but by his raising rents $10 a month per pad now $12,480 even taking out the pad he was living on), Marsh's trailer park should have brought roughly $62,400 in a sale, $17,400 more than he paid for it. And the elapsed time was less than six months!

Marsh held his trailer park for two more years. Each year he raised his rent $2.50 per pad per month, a figure that tenants were willing to pay since it was reasonable. During the entire period he had no vacancy factor, and he plowed back some of the money he made on increased rents into building a small recreation hall. Since most of the tenants were elderly, he felt a swimming pool would have been a waste of time. Also, he gradually made significant improvements in the pathways, roads, and landscaping. When he sold, a cost factor of 6 was used because his trailer park was now much more desirable. His rents were then $40 per pad per month for a total of $13,920 annually, making for a sales price of roughly $84,000. He got it.

While his income had gone up appreciably, his expenses had remained roughly the same, and the next buyer felt he was getting a good deal—which he was. For Marsh, the sale meant a profit of more than $40,000 on a $20,000 investment in less than three years. He went looking for another trailer park.

Before leaving the subject of trailer parks, a word should be said about a disadvantage inherent in them. In our example, which is an actual case, Marsh, who was a postal clerk, had no large income outside his trailer park to worry about. I say "worry" because I am speaking in terms of tax shelter. If Marsh had been making $50,000 a year or more, the trailer park conceivably would not have been as good a deal. Because the majority of the investment is in *land*, there is not a great deal to depreciate on a trailer park; hence there is little tax shelter available. In preparing his tax returns Marsh depreciated the pads, the roads, the utility structures, and eventually the recreational hall. To avoid problems at tax time, it is a good practice to specify in escrow what portion of the purchase price is for improvements, what portion for land, and what for personal property. This was enough tax write-off to keep him from paying any appreciable tax on his yearly profit, but it would not provide additional shelter for other income, something someone who was paying straight tax on $50,000 a year would be greatly concerned about. An apartment building would be a much better choice for such an individual. (Note: See Chapter 8 for an explanation of tax shelters.)

APARTMENT BUILDINGS

I rate these as a good real estate investment for the experienced investor, but a risky venture for someone *totally* new to investing. The opportunity for profit is great, the risk factor is moderate to low, and the leverage can be quite large. In addition, there can be good opportunities for tax shelters in apartment buildings.

Apartments come in all sizes, shapes, and colors. Let us start with the simplest kind, the duplex. This is an apartment particularly popular on the West Coast and combines the benefits of home ownership with income-producing residential property.

Duplexes

A duplex is simply two rental units built together. A triplex is three, a fourplex four. More than four and you have what is commonly called an apartment building. The reason that there is a distinction made for the two-, three-, and four-unit sizes is that most often the purchaser here plans to live in one unit while renting out the remainder. While we shall talk primarily about duplexes, the same principles apply on buildings up to four units.

The duplex is a safe way of investing your money in real estate, but I have never heard of anyone who made a great deal of profit on a duplex. It may seem that it would be an ideal setup to have two units side by side, with you the owner living in one and there all the time to handle any management problems from the rental, but a duplex actually combines the worst of both worlds instead of the best. A duplex unit is not a house. It is not as large or as comfortable. It has a smaller lot, generally speaking, and a smaller garage, and it lacks the one advantage that all houses have, privacy.

From the point of view of the tenant who will rent one half of the duplex, there are also several disadvantages. First, the owner will always be one thin wall away. Although there is very little privacy in any apartment building, there is anonymity in large developments. In these the neighbor next door is also a tenant, in the same situation and likely to understand tenant problems. In a duplex, the neighbor, who is the owner, is much less understanding.

Although duplex owners always claim total occupancy, after many years in renting and buying and selling them my experience is that the average duplex will be vacant from one to two months out of every year. The reasons vary, but usually they are that the owner wants "just the right tenant"; after all, they will be living next door to each other. And it takes "just the right tenant" to be willing to submit to an owner's constant scrutiny. No matter how unassuming the owner may be, it is, after all, his property and he wants to know what is happening to it.

Of course, thus far we are assuming that owner and tenant are compatible. Woe unto the owner who finds a tenant he can't stand. I have seen duplexes where the tenant has literally torn the fixtures from the kitchen wall, broken the windows, and put holes in the walls before moving out, just to spite the owner.

From a financial point of view, buying a duplex is much the same as buying a house. Much the same financing is available, and the qualifying is similar. In some cases a larger down payment may be required, for the very best loans (PMIs) are often not available on duplexes. A duplex does offer the owner certain tax advantages. That portion which he rents out may be depreciated and any expenses incurred in maintaining the rented side can generally be deducted. Of course, as in the case of a home, the owner can write off all interest and taxes.

Full-Size Apartments

These are rental buildings purchased with the exclusive intention of producing income. Before discussing the advantages of different types of apartments, a word must be said about the great disadvantage inherent in all apartment-building ownership, management, and maintenance.

Owning an apartment building is much like nursing a sick relative. There will be constant complaints, and no matter what you do to help, it will never be enough and will never be appreciated. In an apartment building of ten units you can expect constant complaints about air conditioners that do not cool, heaters that do not heat, windows that do not open, and doors that do not close. In an older apartment building you have the additional problems of leaking water heaters, peeling paint, cracking cement, and leaking roofs. If you have ever owned a house, multiply all the things that ever went wrong by 10 (and then by 5 more because a tenant is not going to let as many things pass as you did), and you will get some idea of the maintenance problem with a ten-unit apartment building.

I once handled the renting and eventual sale of a fifteen-apartment-building complex with eleven units in each building. All the buildings were brand-new and supposedly should have had no maintenance problems. Yet from the first day unbelievable things happened. The electrical wiring in the building was all insulated in metal conduit. In one of the buildings the plumbing contractor had somehow connected a cold-water pipe to an open electrical conduit. The first day the water was connected water poured from light fixtures, sockets, and switches throughout the building. And the building had been passed by all building inspectors! Later a stairway sagged and had to be replaced. Brand-new carpeting in several units wore out in less than two months. The list was endless.

In addition, there is the problem of renting vacant units and vacating units where tenants refuse to pay rent. If you own an apartment building, you can safely assume that each time a tenant moves out, regardless of how long the stay was, you will have to do some repainting, carpet cleaning, and general washing and fixing up. Once these are done, you will have to pay advertising costs, and when prospective tenants come by, you (or a manager whom you will have to pay) will have to be available to show the vacant unit. Here a little salesmanship is in order, but even when the future tenant is satisfied with the unit and wants to rent it, you will have to make certain checks on his character and credit to be confident that he can and will pay the rent.

A common misconception of many who have not had experience in renting property is that they can gain added protection against a bad tenant by insisting on a lease. In actual fact a lease does not protect the owner of residential property—it protects the tenant. The lease guarantees that (1) you will not raise the rent until a specified point in time, and (2) you will not sell the building out from under the tenant and force him or her to move without giving adequate notice and in certain cases compensation.

A lease in most states does not allow you to sue the tenant who moves out and refuses to pay rent *until that rent becomes due*. If he moves in on a one-year lease and moves out after one month, you can only sue him each month as his rent becomes due for the amount unpaid or wait the entire year and then sue for the full amount. Your chances of collecting await the interpretation of the court and the solvency of the tenant. In the meantime, your apartment remains vacant. In many cases, owners who have found themselves in this predicament find it cheaper and easier to simply rerent the apartment as soon as possible and take the loss. (Note: If you rerent the apartment and receive income from it, in many cases you must subtract this from the amount of money owed by the tenant who defaulted on the lease.)

But the worst managerial problem of all comes from the tenant who will neither pay nor leave. Although years ago it was possible to hire a few strong men to come in and get such a tenant out on the street, excesses in such acts have led to legislation in virtually all states providing strict rules for eviction. Usually a written notice must be given. Then, court aid (with legal expense) must be sought and an eviction notice obtained. Often a bond must be put up either to ensure that when the tenant is evicted, no harm will come to his or her possessions or to ensure that the city, whose police usually handle such evictions, will not have to pay storage on evicted personal property that a tenant does not claim. An eviction today can cost anywhere from a minimum of $150 to $500, depending on the area and the incident. And in some states, if the tenant happens to be a woman living alone who is beyond her sixth month of pregnancy, you cannot remove her without her consent until her child is born. If you do and for any reason the child is born defective or the mother is injured, you may be liable for a big lawsuit.

Those are the disadvantages. The advantages take a much shorter space to describe: tax shelter and the potential of enormous profit. To get a good example of how much profit can be made (and how management headaches can be minimized with careful planning) check out Howard and Gail VanTill's story in Chapter 2.

Apartment buildings fall into three categories depending on the rental income received: buildings with high-, medium-, and moderate-income units.

Moderate-Income Apartments These are rarely built today by individuals for profit because there is virtually no profit in them. Land is costly, construction is costly, and taxes are high. It is not really possible to make a decent profit on moderate-income housing unless you build or buy under one of the government's moderate-income housing programs. A number are available under the Department of Housing and Urban Development (HUD).

The advantages of these programs are that some of them provide enormous tax write-offs in the first years, in most cases there is no recapture of depreciation after the project is ten years old, and if the sale proceeds are reinvested in a similar project, it is possible to defer the tax.

The disadvantages are equally great. Usually there are high operating expenses, vandalism is often high, and tenants may be slow in paying rents or may simply be unable or unwilling to pay at all.

There are basically three programs available. The most popular is section 236.

Section 236 works in this fashion: the investor (or group of investors) puts up a down payment, and the government then guarantees a forty-year loan for up to 90 percent of the project cost to a private lender. In addition, the government provides for a monthly rent-subsidy payment directly to the lender. The formula for the subsidy is fairly complicated, but basically it is that the government will make up the difference in interest between a mortgage at 1 percent per year and the current normal mortgage rate—up to HUD limitations. It requires, however, that the savings in interest be passed on as lower rents and not taken as profit.

The big limitation on section 236 has to do with profits. The group that sets out to develop such a project is termed a "profit-making limited dividend entity," which means, in effect, that after payment of mortgage interest and principal, expenses, reserve funds, etc., the cash distributed back to the investors cannot exceed 6 percent of the initial investment of each partner as defined by the FHA. (In most cases the FHA definition of the equity investment is smaller than the actual investment.)

But the big incentive to the investor is the tax shelter. For example, assume that a million-dollar project is being built. The loan is $850,-000, and five investors are putting up $30,000 apiece for the remaining $150,000. The return to investors might look as indicated in Table 9-2.

Table 9-2. Typical 236 FHA Programs, in thousands

	Investment	Cash return (estimated)	Estimated loss (in parentheses) or taxable income	Tax savings in 50% tax bracket	Tax savings in 70% tax bracket
1975	$10	....	($9)	$4.5	$ 6.3
1976	10	$0.9	(14)	7.0	9.8
1977	10	0.9	(17)	8.5	11.9
1978		0.9	(13)	6.5	9.1
1979		0.8	(9)	4.5	6.3
1980		0.8	(8)	4.0	5.6
1981		0.8	(8)	4.0	5.6
1982		0.8	(7)	3.5	4.9
1983		0.8	(6)	3.0	4.2
1984		0.8	(5)	2.5	3.5
1985		0.8	(4)	2.0	2.8
1986		0.8	(3)	1.5	2.1
1987		0.8	(2)	1.0	1.4
1988		0.8	(1)	0.5	0.7
1989		0.8	(1)	0.5	0.7
1990		0.8	(1)	0.5	0.7
1991		0.8	(1)	0.5	0.7
1992		0.8	1	—	—
1993		0.8	1	—	—
1994		0.8	1	—	—
1995		0.8	2	—	—

We can conclude the following from Table 9-2: The investor in the 50 percent tax bracket during the first year will have to put up $10,000 in cash but will immediately get back a tax shelter worth $4,500 at income tax time. The second and third years he will only have to put up $9,100 each year because he will be receiving back tax-free spendable income of $900 from the investment. In addition, the second year he will receive a shelter worth $7,000 and the third year a shelter worth $8,500. This means that he will recoup his total investment by the fifth year and continue to receive tax-free spendable income plus shelter until the seventeenth year, at which time he will have to start paying taxes on the small income. The investor in the 70 percent tax bracket will do even better. He will recoup his total investment by the fourth year, and his shelter will be proportionately larger.

If everything goes well, after the end of twenty years he can sell the building to a co-op of tenants and defer payment of any tax on the proceeds, provided he reinvests in a similar project within a limited time period. He can continue to defer his taxes by buying into, and selling, new projects until he dies and thereby escape the tax. That is, if everything goes well.

If it does not, he could be in big trouble, taxwise. If vandalism is abnormally high or if tenants in larger than expected numbers refuse or are unable to pay rent or if any of a dozen other variables go against him, the project can fail and the loan be foreclosed upon. If this happens before the ten-year minimum to forgive accelerated depreciation, the investor can suddenly find that a good portion of the depreciation above 100 percent (it was figured on the accelerated basis of 200 percent) coming back at him in the year of foreclosure (sale) as regular income. In the 50 percent tax bracket he would now have to pay 50 percent of this figure in tax, in the 70 percent bracket 70 percent in tax!

Or, at the time he sells the project after the twenty years, he might not want to invest in another high-risk venture such as this. In that case he would have to pay a substantial tax on his profits.

In general this program is good for someone who anticipates being in a high tax bracket for at least five years and who is willing to run a few risks for a huge shelter.

The two other sections available are 221(d)(3) and 221(d)(4). Section 221(d)(3) is basically the same as 236 except that there are no reductions in the interest payment and each of the rental units receives a supplement payment from the rent-supplement program. Section 221(d)(4) is different from 236 in that there is no interest-payment subsidy and no rental subsidy, although the FHA still insures the loan up to 90 percent of the project cost. Under this program, rentals may be higher, but are subject to controls; profits are not subject to controls.

Medium-Income Apartments   These are probably the best bet in real estate investment in apartments during the seventies. We have had a housing boom in this country for almost thirty years, and apartments have been built during most of that time. It is possible without too great a difficulty to find an *older* building, purchase it, and make a significant profit.

But I would stay away from newer buildings. There was a fad, mentioned in the first part of this chapter, a few years ago of building and then selling new medium-income apartment projects. The reason for the fad was that financing and land were readily available. In a typical case, a developer would buy a parcel of land, putting one-fourth to one-third down and giving the original owner a first loan which that owner agreed to subordinate to a construction loan. The developer would then get two loans. He would go to a large lending institution, a savings and loan, insurance company, mortgage banking company, or bank and ask for a "take-out" loan. This loan the lending institution would give *after* the building was completed. Let us say, for example, that the developer wanted to build a ten-unit building at a cost of $120,000. The lending institution would say that at the end of a specified period of time, say one year, it would loan $120,000 at 8 percent interest for a term of twenty years, *provided* the building was completed. It usually also insisted on holding back 20 percent of the money until a certain rental occupancy figure was established, usually 90 percent. The developer would then go to a bank (or it could be the same lending institution) and obtain a construction loan. This would give him the money he needed to construct the building. Now it was all a gamble on time.

It was ordinarily easy enough to finish a building within six months. That left the developer six months to get it 90 percent occupied and obtain the full take-out loan. In the meantime he very often had plans of selling the structure at a large profit.

Two things have gone wrong with this plan in recent years. First, new medium-income apartments were terribly overbuilt in many suburban areas. Just as was the case in new trailer parks, the builder-developers invariably went to the edge of metropolitan areas where land was cheap to construct new housing. This normally would not be a problem in most areas because they hoped to attract young, working people as potential tenants, those who could be expected to drive fairly long distances and would not be expected to object to living away from center cities. However, too many buildings were constructed at once, and those which were completed suddenly ran into vacancy factors as high as 25 percent. Developers were giving as much as three months free rent to tenants to induce them to move in.

At the end of the year when the builder got his take-out loan, 20 percent was held back because the buildings were not 90 percent occupied. Here the second damaging factor entered. The enormous rate of inflation in the past few years has sent the cost of construction material and labor soaring. Almost without exception, every project that had been estimated to cost one price cost at least 10 percent more after six months. When the take-out-loan lender withheld 20 percent of $120,000, or $24,000, this ate not only into the developer's profit but into his construction costs. Without putting up more capital, he could not pay off his construction loan or his workers. Since most builders work on very small capital reserves, the number of foreclosures on new moderate income apartments in recent years has been astonishing. In 1972 out of some 6,000 starts in the five Western states alone, nearly 3,300 were either in foreclosure or threatened with foreclosure one year later. Needless to say, lending institutions are shying away from *new* medium-income apartments.

However, there are numerous older apartment buildings available. Using the same strategy as was described for trailer parks, it is possible to find older medium-income apartment units in good areas near the centers of town these days and make a profit on them. As with the trailer parks, these were built at the cities' outskirts twenty years ago, and the cities have simply grown around them. Often they have been neglected and the rents are low. Here again a cost factor of from 5 to 7 times gross income applies, and it is possible to pick such apartment buildings up cheaply, renovate, raise rents, and sell at a profit.

These investments differ in several ways from trailer parks. It is much more difficult to renovate an older apartment house than it is a trailer park. Although it is often overlooked by anxious investors, the biggest problem is one of style. An older building reflects the architectural trends of the era in which it was built. You can repaint, refinish, recarpet, retile, replumb, and put in new appliances and still a building that was constructed in 1947 looks like a building that was constructed in 1947.

However, the location of many of these older apartment buildings offsets this disadvantage. In the newer downtown areas they are convenient to shopping, recreation, transportation, and the excitement of city life. And finally, their biggest advantage is their low rent.

Even though a building you buy may look like 1947, if you can rent a modernized one-bedroom apartment for $175 a month and the apartment building next door which was constructed a year ago has to charge $250 for the same space because of increased building costs, then you are going to have a very low vacancy factor. In fact, a well-located medium-income apartment building that is not overcharging on rents can reasonably expect a 3 to 5 percent vacancy factor (as compared with 15 or 25 percent in the suburbs).

It takes looking, but older, run-down apartment buildings where the rents are low and hence the price is low can be found. And if you find one, it will undoubtedly benefit you to buy it.

Financing is the key to buying apartment buildings. My advice is to put down more cash if your income is low, less cash if it is high. Let us take the case of Harold Fieldman, who purchased an eleven-unit building on Goldeen Street for $125,000. His deal looked like this:

Price	$125,000	
Down	$10,000	
First loan	$90,000	at 10% from a savings and loan for twenty-five years at $900 a month
Second loan	$25,000	taken back by owner for ten years at 9% payable $250 per month—balloon payment at tenth year

Mr. Fieldman had heard that leverage was the key to purchasing real estate and that the less money of his he put into a building, the more profit he could expect.

The income of the building was figured at roughly $24,000 a year. It had one-bedroom units rented out at $180 a month. Since Mr. Fieldman had bought with a cost factor of 6, he felt that he had gotten a bargain. In fact he had. It is not that easy to get eleven units for $125,000 in any condition these days. However, he had figured poorly in his financing.

His first loan cost him $900 a month, or roughly $11,000 annually. His second cost him $250 a month, or $3,000 annually. His taxes were $6,000 a year. The figures added up to this:

First loan	$11,000
Second loan	3,000
Taxes	6,000
Total	$20,000

He added in no maintenance or management charge because he planned to live in one of the apartments and take care of the place himself.

However, his income figure had not taken into consideration a vacancy factor of 5 percent, which reduced it from $24,000 to $22,800 a year Nor had he reckoned that since he would be occupying one of the apartments as his own residence, he would have to subtract an additional $180 per month, $2,160 per year, from income. Now his income looked like this:

Total anticipated	$24,000
Less 5% vacancy	1,200
Less residence	2,160
Actual total	$20,640

When he added in the cost of garbage service, water (which he paid on all the units), a business license which happened to be required of owners of residential units of more than eight units in the city he was in, and normal upkeep and maintenance that he could not handle (such as the cost of a new water heater, the repair of a broken window, a new stove) he found it was costing him an additional $2,900 a year. Add this to the $20,000 fixed expenses, and he was actually having to take $2,260 a year out of his pocket just to maintain the building.

Of course with all the expenses and the loss, Mr. Fieldman had an excellent tax write-off. It went something like this:

Interest on loans	$11,000	a year (approx.)
Taxes	6,000	
Depreciation	8,000	building valued at $80,000 depreciated 200% over twenty years
Maintenance	2,900	
	$27,900	

As explained in Chapter 8 under tax shelters, Mr. Fieldman could now subtract the $27,900 from his income on the property of $20,640. This gave him a loss for tax purposes of $7,260 which under current tax laws he normally could deduct from any other income. Unfortunately he did not have an unusually high income. He regularly made only $15,000 a year on which he paid about $2,500 after taking normal deductions including the taxes and interest on the house he had formerly owned. Now, of course, he could deduct the $7,260 from this regular income, reducing it to $7,740 on which he only had to pay about $1,400 in taxes This was a savings of $1,100 which helped to offset the cash loss on the apartment building. Now it was only costing him $1,160 a year out of his pocket to keep the property.

Deductions	$27,900
Income	20,640
Tax loss	$ 7,260
Regular income	$15,000
Less tax loss	7.260
Reduced income	$ 7,740

But let's consider what would happen if Mr. Fieldman were in a higher tax bracket. Let's assume his regular income is $50,000 a year. As a single person he is close to a 60 percent tax bracket. Out of every dollar he can deduct from his income, he can save 60¢ which would otherwise be paid in tax. On the building's $7,260 tax loss, he can save about $4,300—enough to offset the actual cash loss on the property and show a cash, tax-free profit of $2,096 or better than a 20 percent return on his $10,000 investment!

But what if our Mr. Fieldman had stuck $30,000 into the property instead of $10,000? His return could have looked like this:

EXPENSES:	$11,000	
First loan only	6,000	
Taxes	6,000	
Maintenance	2,900	
Total	$19,900	
INCOME	20,640	
Profit	$ 740	
TAX EVALUATION:		
Deductions:		
Interest on loan	$ 9,000	(No second mortgage)
Taxes	6,000	
Depreciation	8,000	
Maintenance	2,900	
Total	$25,900	
Less Income	20,640	
Excess loss	$ 5,260	

The excess loss would reduce Mr. Fieldman's regular income and thereby his regular tax, saving him about $700 in cash. When this amount is added to the $740 in profit on the building we show a total gain of $1,400, a little less than a 5 percent return on his investment. While this may seem a small return, I am sure Mr. Fieldman would feel a lot better about it than the cash loss of $1,140 it was costing him when he only invested $10,000. (And don't forget, in both cases he is living rent-free!)

One last very important point. This whole hypothetical apartment case was built on the premise that the 5 percent vacancy factor remained constant. If it had jumped to 10 percent, it would have wiped out the Mr. Fieldman who only invested $10,000, while a Mr. Fieldman who had invested $30,000 would be hurt somewhat but would remain solvent. This echoes my feeling on apartment buildings. If your regular income is relatively low, do not take chances with high-leverage, low-down-payment deals. They are risky. If your income is high and you can write off a lot of depreciation—that is to say, you need a good tax shelter—put a little down.

High-Rent Apartments Unless you have a lot of money and a lot of experience (in which case you don't need to read this book), stay away from these. High-rent apartment buildings have rentals anywhere from $400 a month on up past $1,500 a month. One recent development in a suburban area of Los Angeles offered rents beginning at $1,800 per month including maid service and meals.

A high-rent apartment is usually a well-planned project built by skilled developers. There are not that many people around who can pay large rents; consequently each building has to have a solid chance of success. Often lending institutions are themselves part owners of such projects.

The average real estate investor usually gets into such a deal only as a partner in a syndication of a high-rent building. If you happen to be in this position, I would say that the key factors to take into consideration are the desirability of the apartment project to tenants and the availability of suitable qualified renters.

Almost assuredly the project will be in an exclusive section of a city and probably near other high-rent projects. The proposed development should, however, be unique. At high rents the tenant can afford to be snobbish. Often the snob appeal will attract renters. On the other hand, if the apartment building for one reason or another gets a bad reputation, vacancy factors of more than 50 percent can develop. And lowering the rents will not help here!

High-rent apartments, while potentially the most profitable of all apartment developments, are also the riskiest, particularly during a recession. If you invest in one, you can hope for the moon in profits, but be ready to lose your shirt.

BARE LAND

This form of real estate investment is not as popular today as it was a few years ago. Probably there have been too many stories of investors who have "taken a bath" in raw land deals. While it is undoubtedly true that some have lost their money investing this way, it is equally true that fortunes have been made. In land, quite often the owner of the large parcel who subdivides into smaller parcels does very well indeed, and the small speculator who buys the smaller parcels takes a beating.

In order to understand the theory of land investing, it is well to harken back to the first and possibly the greatest land investor America (and possibly the world) has ever known, John Jacob Astor. When Astor died in 1848, he was the richest man in America and one of the five or six richest men in the world. His success can be attributed in large part to his shrewd buying of bare land.

Astor's story is what many have claimed inspired the fictional Horatio Alger stories. Astor arrived in America virtually penniless, an immigrant from Germany. He worked for a time selling bread for a German baker, then went to work for a furrier. Within a year he learned all he had to know and went into the fur business. Borrowing money from his brother Henry, he opened a small music store, which his wife managed while he went into the northern wilderness to buy pelts from Indians. Within a few short years he amassed a fortune of some $250,000, an enormous sum in 1800. It was then that he began to think about real estate investment.

As historians tell it, Astor did not buy his first lot until he was thirty-seven years old. He bought it in Manhattan, which then had a population of less than 50,000. New York was the hub of commerce for the East Coast, and Astor reckoned correctly that it had to grow. His "secret of success," which was no secret at all, was a method which all businessmen of the era were aware of but Astor took advantage of. It was based on two convictions: First, Manhattan, with its natural harbor and access to the interior of the country, had to grow. Second, since the city was then limited to the southern tip of Manhattan Island, the only direction it could grow was north. Astor simply went beyond the edges of the city into goat pastures and marshland and bought as many lots as he could. Then he waited. Within a few short years the city of New York, ever expanding, came to his property, and what he had paid $100 or $200 for he sold for $1,000 or $2,000. Although this ratio of profit (1,000 percent) may seem enormous, it is in fact quite accurate. The worse deal Astor ever made reportedly was on some land he bought in upstate New York. He sold it for only 25 percent profit within two years and lamented the poor return to his deathbed.

There is an oft-told story of Astor that bears repeating, for it casts light on the man and his thinking. Astor had a lot near Wall Street which he agreed to sell to another investor for a price reported to be $8,000. When the sale concluded, the man came to Astor and laughingly said, "Why John, you have finally made a poor land deal. In a few years this lot which you sold me for $8,000 will be worth $12,000." "That's true," Astor is said to have replied, "but with the $8,000 you have given me I will buy eighty lots above Canal Street. Within the few years it takes your property to be worth $12,000 my eighty lots will be worth $80,000." The story ends by saying that Astor was correct.

In addition to buying lots, Astor made it a practice to lease them out to tenants who constructed buildings on them. He would then use the rent money to purchase new lots. Whether it is true or not remains a matter of speculation, but historians record that Astor never borrowed money to buy any real estate, but always paid cash. The result of this was that when the panic of 1837 and the subsequent depression hit, he was barely affected, losing only some rental income.

It is an interesting sidelight to the Astor story that the parcel of land he made his small 25 percent profit on in upstate New York he sold to his brother George, who lived in London. He assured George, who never saw the land, that it was a good investment and that in a few years it would double in value. George, seeing John's immense success in real estate, believed him and bought. Some thirty years later, when George had died and his executors were trying to settle the estate, they could find no buyers for the property and eventually had to sell it for 12¢ on the dollar.

Just as with John Jacob Astor, success in bare-land investing comes from buying cheaply in outlying areas and then waiting for cities to move in. However, Astor had one advantage that most investors lack. He was buying on Manhattan Island and the *only* direction the city could go was north. Rarely has any other city offered such guarantees. Most investors have to take a gamble on which direction cities will grow. Some guess correctly, and some do not.

Another important concept to keep in mind when dealing with bare land is that the land itself had no inherent value whatever. It is only the *use* the land is put to that makes it valuable. It can be used for mining, agricultural, residential, commercial, or industrial purposes. Each type of use has a different value. For example, in general any residential use makes the land more valuable than any agricultural use. And any commercial use makes it more valuable than any residential use. And no use at all makes it totally worthless, except to the tax assessor. If you are thinking of buying land in the hinterlands of Oregon or the desert of New Mexico, keep in mind that if you cannot put the land to *some use immediately*, it will just sit there producing no income and costing you taxes.

This is not to say that because a parcel of land is away from a city it is worthless. Land in the mountains, by lakes, or even in the desert near established vacation communities can have extremely high value. Palm Springs in California and the recently developed Lake Havasu in Arizona are examples of land achieving high residential value because of its vacation-resort potential.

Finally, there is the matter of land speculation. Land investment, by nature, tends to be highly speculative, and over the course of our history there have been enumerable "land booms." Perhaps the most famous is the land boom of the 1920s in Florida.

Miami, Palm Beach, and St. Augustine boomed largely because of the efforts of a developer named Henry Morrison Flagler. Flagler made his money as a partner with John D. Rockefeller in a firm that eventually became known as Standard Oil Company of Ohio. Flagler came to Florida in the late 1880s for his health and fell in love with the climate. Florida then was relatively inaccessible to all but the hardiest of travelers. Flagler changed all this by building a railroad, eventually all the way to Miami. (He had plans to go all the way to Key West, but they did not work out, and the railroad line he built—called the East Coast Railway—became the basis for the interisland highway.) As Flagler moved his rail line south from St. Augustine, he bought land and built vacation-resort hotels. Wealthy people from the East Coast, wanting to get away from winter snows, swarmed south to these areas, and Flagler became immensely successful.

The Florida chambers of commerce, seeing a gold mine in the resort trade, advertised it heavily in Eastern publications. With the many vacationers came a few speculators who saw that land values were doubling every few years as the trade increased. They bought heavily and sold quickly for profits. It is an axiom that where there are large amounts of money to be made, you can't keep the news a secret for very long. Word got out that a man with a relatively small amount of money could make a fortune overnight in Florida. Now almost as many speculators as vacationers were coming down, and the era of wild speculation began.

Whereas until 1920 the price of land kept fairly close to its usage for vacation areas, the price was made to bound upward by speculators who gambled on future value. It was not uncommon for a lot that had been worth $100 on Monday to be sold on Wednesday for $200 and on Friday for $500, and quite often the persons who bought for the $100 on Monday and the $200 on Wednesday never had to put up a dime. They did not close their escrows until the last person put up the $500 on Friday in cash. Of course, this person was counting on selling the land for $1,000 the following Monday!

Wild speculation creates a kind of nightmarish pyramid where cost has no relationship to actual value. As long as there are more and more people willing to spend ever-greater sums of money on the land, everyone does well. But when the day comes that one last speculator cannot be found to pay the one last boost in price, the whole pyramid caves in. When the Friday person could not find somebody to buy the property for $1,000 on Monday, it was necessary to lower the price— first to $950, then $900, then $750, then to break even at $500, and finally to take anything anyone would offer. But since the person who sold for $100 had bought it for $50 from someone who bought the land for $25 from someone who bought it for $5 from someone who could not understand why anyone would pay more than 25¢ for swampland that was under water, no buyers could be found and everything was lost.

Much land investment to a greater or lesser degree is like this. If you buy low and sell high during an artificial boom, you can make a fortune. But if you guess wrong about location or are the last person on the pyramid during a boom, you will be wiped out.

The most common land deals today that the small investor is likely to run into are those advertised in the paper as something like "ideal vacation homes." Often they are hundreds of miles away from any metropolitan area, and as an added inducement to purchase them, the seller will occasionally pay for a jet flight to and from the location for prospective purchasers. When it comes time to purchase the property, a small down payment is asked, with relatively small monthly payments over an extended period of time. A not uncommon advertisement is $50 down and $50 a month.

Are these good land deals or bad? The answer really depends on what you are looking for. Assuming that the seller is honest and will in fact grant you clear title after you have paid an agreed-upon portion of the full price, the worst you could do would be to end up with a vacation spot a few hundred miles from home. If this is what you want and particularly if your site is near a lake or fishing stream, mountains, or a desert or some other recreational area, it could be an excellent investment for you. However, if your intention is to buy, hold a short time, and then sell for profit, watch out. Here is why.

There is very little leverage possible on bare-land deals. Ordinarily banks and most other lending institutions will not even touch them. And no lending institutions will loan on "wilderness" land. Yet it stands to reason that the promoters of a "new city in the wilderness" are not likely to get people to put down, for example, $3,000 on a $3,000 lot out in the wilds of northern California. (Yes, northern California does still have wilds.) What they will in fact do, very often, is purchase a large tract of land, say 400 acres, for a few hundred dollars an acre. Perhaps there is a stream running through part of the land which they will advertise as an inducement to future purchasers. Then they will divide the 400 acres into lots of perhaps ¼ acre apiece. If they do this, they now have 4 times 400, or 1,600, lots to sell. The price is arbitrary. They will ask as much as they think they can get. If the land is in the Sierras, not too steep yet with a mountain atmosphere, and they have done some grading, put in some improved or dirt roads, and made utilities available, they might choose to ask $5,000 a lot. This is, in fact, rather low for even poor mountain property today. If they paid $500 an acre for 400 acres, or $200,000, and spent another $100,000 on improvements and advertising, they have over a quarter-million-dollar investment. But if they were to sell all 1,600 lots at $5,000 a lot, they would stand to make the phenomenal sum of $8,000,000.

Although there are few mountain developments of such size and most legitimate ones ask for at least one-fourth down, our developers could go the 50-50 route. For $50 down and $50 a month they could give a buyer a *land contract of sale*. This should not be confused with a deed. Basically this is a contract to purchase a piece of property at a specified *future* time. Most such contracts read that after the buyer has paid one-fourth or more of the purchase price plus interest, the seller will issue him a deed and either finance the balance himself or allow the purchaser to secure his own financing. On a 50-50 deal it can be several years before the buyer even gets title to the property.

The contract-of-sale agreement contains disadvantages for the buyer. In most states such an agreement can provide that if the buyer does not make the payments or fulfill other terms *exactly* as specified, the seller can declare the deal null and void and keep any moneys thus far paid as a forfeiture. In California, for example, if a buyer obtains a piece of property in the normal fashion with a loan on it, he takes title and issues a promissory note for the loan amount and a deed of trust. If he defaults, there are prescribed procedures which take on the average about four to six months through which the seller, or holder of the loan, must go before he can get property back. In other states that use mortgages, the seller, or morgagee, must go through court to get the property. On a contract of sale, the seller can simply fail to give the buyer a deed and then go out and resell the property to someone else. It becomes the burden of the purchaser to take the seller to court to prove that he has in fact lived up to all agreements in the contract of sale and is entitled to a deed. Although in recent years the courts have given some protection to holders of contracts of sale such as the right to record such documents with only the buyer's signature notarized, they are still the shakiest of all vehicles for purchasing property.

There are a few protections that buyers of raw land have. The Land

Sales Full Disclosure Act applies if the seller plans to sell fifty or more lots *interstate*. He must file a report with HUD. The report must contain as many as twenty-eight significant facts about the development. It may include such things as planned facilities, the general nature of the land, the length of time before installations will be made, the availability of water, sewer facilities, and the existence of liens (mortgages) on the property. He must show this report to all buyers. If he does not, the buyer conceivably has a case for declaring a purchase contract null and void. On the other hand, if the seller does in fact describe the property as it is and shows the description to the buyer, he has met the HUD requirements. He does not have to say whether he is offering a good deal or a bad one; he must only describe accurately the deal offered.

Many states go further and require prospective sellers to file subdivision reports with real estate departments. California, for example, requires that any parcel of land subdivided into five or more sections must have a subdivision report under the California Subdivision Map Act. The state then investigates the subdivision and proposed sale terms and, if the facts are as stated and there is no fraud or attempt at misrepresentation, issues its own report, which must be shown to a buyer. On several occasions the state has prevented the development of subdivisions because of misstatements of facts. Unfortunately, the law applies only to parcels under 160 acres in size.

The most solid land deal is where the buyer goes out, finds a piece of land he likes for whatever reason, and either pays cash or makes a substantial down payment on it. He does this with the understanding that this is a *long-term* investment that may or may not bring profit in the distant future. The investor who tries to get in on a land boom becomes a speculator in a speculative market. One must get in low and get out before the crash. It can be done, but usually it is only done successfully by those who spend their lives watching the market. A good rule of thumb is that if you have to ask someone else's advice on when to get in and when to get out, stay out. You do not know enough to be in the game. In general, during boom periods or times of rapid expansion, land price increases lead the field. During recessions, land often becomes difficult if not impossible to sell (unless it is severely discounted).

CONDOMINIUMS

These are still probably the most popular item for builders, and well they should be. A builder can put up a well-made four-unit building for $100,000 today, but the chances of finding a single buyer for such a piece of property are slim. The return on four units for $100,000 is low, and the cash required to make the purchase is high. On the other hand, one can call it a condominium and sell each unit individually for $25,000. There are a lot more people willing to spend $25,000 than $100,000. In addition, through government FHA financing the buyer can get in with as little as 3 percent down payment. All the builder has to do is find four buyers to get the original investment and the profit on it out of the deal. There are no rental headaches, no worry about getting 90 percent occupancy in order to get a full take-out loan, no concern about tying money up in a building for an extended period of time.

For the buyers a "condo" can be a good deal too, provided it is *well located*. Condominiums provide many of the advantages of owning a house without the problems of upkeep. Usually a set fee is paid every month by each owner, and someone is hired to handle maintenance. Many modern condominiums have swimming pools and, in the large units, recreation halls. All that the buyer really sacrifices in comparison with a house is a little privacy and, sometimes, a little living area. (Most "condos" are smaller than homes.) But the buyer gains in terms of a lower price. Some two-bedroom condominium units sell for under $15,000, with less than 5 percent down. Where can you find a new two-bedroom house today for $15,000?

One problem with condominiums that is usually underemphasized is that monthly maintenance fee. It has a nasty habit of going up, particularly as the building gets older. It has to take care of water heaters and broken windows and other repairs. It also has to cover the rising costs of the labor hired to maintain the buildings.

As a place to live for people who want this type of life, condominiums are an excellent investment. As the old argument that real estate people frequently use goes, "It's better than paying rent." When you decide to move, you sell and get most of your money back. If you rent a comparable apartment, all the money you pay is gone.

As an investment, a "condo" is good only if the property is going to appreciate rapidly. Since most condominiums are fairly new, it is difficult to make improvements that will increase value. Also, since prospective buyers usually buy only one unit, there is little they can do individually to boost the value. They have to wait for the entire building to go up in price.

Condominiums that are built in downtown areas where living expenses are high or that are built by vacation areas tend to rise faster in value because of demand than the surrounding area. One recent exception occurred with the 1974 oil embargo. Several condominiums that I am familiar with in Palm Springs actually declined slightly in value because of the problems incurred in getting gasoline to drive there from the Los Angeles area.

"Condos" as rentals face the advantages and problems of renting a cross between a house and an apartment. Depreciation (plus, of course, taxes and interest) can be deducted, giving a modest tax shelter. Generally, tenants are easier to find because the units are bigger and more private than apartments. But they are also harder to find because you usually have to charge a higher rent. I would only suggest buying a condominium as a rental investment if you calculate that it will appreciate dramatically in value in a fairly short time and just want to rent it in order to make loan payments and taxes. That is, you are simply renting it until you can sell for a profit. I do not believe there is much money to be made over a short period of time in renting condominiums.

VACATION HOMES

Many people have dreamed of buying a cabin up in the mountains, renting it out part of the time, and using it the rest of the time themselves. Until 1972 this was a moneymaking proposition. However, in 1972 the Internal Revenue Service (IRS) changed its ruling regarding vacation homes. In general if you used a home any part of a year, even one or two days, as a residence for yourself, you could not depreciate it or claim expenses that would normally be claimed on a rental. What this decision means can be seen in the following example:

Vacation home rented two-thirds of a year

	Old ruling	New procedure
Income from rent	$3,000	$3,000
Interest and taxes	2,700	2,700
Profit	$ 300	$ 300
Maintenance $900, two-thirds business use	$ 600	no deduction allowed
Utilities $300, two-thirds business use	$ 200	no deduction allowed
Depreciation $1,800, two-thirds business use	$1,200	no deduction allowed
Year's taxable loss	$1,700	none ($300 profit taxed as regular income)

Before 1972 this vacation home brought $300 to its owner in tax-free cash and gave a $1,700 tax shelter to apply to other income. After 1972 the same vacation home brought $300 that had to be declared as regular income and on which taxes had to be paid and offered no tax shelter at all.

The IRS has effectively made vacation homes just that. They can no longer be used as a business. If you buy one and plan to rent it out, you have to be sure that it will make enough money to pay for itself. You cannot count on deductions for depreciation, utilities, and maintenance (as Mr. Fieldman did in our earlier example on apartment buildings) to carry you through.

Of course, there is one other alternative and that is to buy a vacation home and only rent it out, never use it yourself. Here all the tax advantages of a real estate investment, including depreciation and deductions for expenses, apply. However, I object to calling such a purchase a "vacation" home. Since the owner never enjoys the premises, never takes a vacation there, it is strictly a business investment in a recreational area. And as such it has certain disadvantages, which include remoteness and tough financing (often 25 to 50 percent of the purchase price must be cash).

The remoteness from the investor's residence usually presents two big problems. The first is difficulty in maintaining the vacation home. Either the investor has to hire someone at the site to take care of it, a risky and uncertain business at best, or she has to be constantly making drives to the property to fix broken windows, unplug drains, etc. The second problem is finding tenants. Since most recreational-type property rents for only a few weeks at a time, the turnover is enormous. And even with tenants leaving substantial deposits, the opportunity for damage through carelessness or vandalism is great. It is all rather like trying to run a one-unit motel without ever being there.

On the plus side is the fact that rents can be much higher than in conventional areas, often twice as high due to the desirability of recreational zones and to the short rental periods. Also, in choice areas, when it comes time to sell there can be a hefty profit.

As in all real estate investments, location is of prime importance. With a vacation home it is indeed everything, if you eventually want to resell for profit. The ideal thing to do is to find an area that has not been built up, buy a vacation home there, and wait for the recreational interest in the area to peak. Does this sound like the same proposition as buying raw land? It is.

HOUSES

These are the very best bet for the beginning investor. If you have to ask why, just reread Chapter 2.

A word should be said, however, about houses as rentals. I have a very close friend who has 23 houses in the San Francisco area. He has bought them over a period of eleven or twelve years and rents them out, all the while continuing to work at his regular job as a produce clerk in a supermarket. I know his story well because I sold him most of his homes.

Jean has a plan. It is a long-term plan for making a fortune in Real Estate and it is working quite well for him thus far. Using all his savings, he buys homes, rents them out and uses whatever profits he gets from his rentals to buy more homes. To my knowledge he has never sold a house that he has bought. He started with less than $2,500 and today his net worth is well in excess of a quarter-million dollars.

His plan operates on this assumption: he will always be able to rent every house for at least the monthly payments, including taxes and maintenance. Since he bought with as little down as possible and has loans which originally were for twenty-five to thirty years, the tenants are paying off his property for him. All he has to do is keep the property rented and in another fifteen or so years he will own twenty-three houses free and clear.

When he bought, because he paid very little down, times were very hard for him. At first he could only rent his houses for just enough money to make payments. But as the years passed the houses increased in market value, and the amount he could charge successfully for rent also increased. Yet, with the exception of taxes, his monthly payments (principal and interest on his loan) remained the same. I sold him the first house he bought. His monthly payment including principal, interest, taxes, and insurance was $108 a month. He rented it out for $112. That only left him $4 a month margin to pay for all repairs and to carry him through periods of vacancy. A risky business. Today, however, nearly twelve years later, that same house is renting for $195 a month. And tax increases have raised his payments only to $132.

Rental income	$195
Fixed monthly payment	132
Remainder	$ 63

He now has $63 to apply toward maintenance and potential vacancies, or roughly one-third of the income. A very substantial margin indeed. Jean now regularly takes over $1,000 a month as profit out of his houses, all the while maintaining sizable reserves for upkeep, vacancy, and refurbishing. He has no intention of selling any of his properties until he gets to be fifty-five, some fourteen years from now. And he says, "I probably won't sell them even then. Hell, by then half'll be paid off and I can live like a king on just the monthly rentals."

If you have the time, Jean's way is probably the safest way to make a fortune in real estate. A recession will not hurt him; only a full-scale depression that would put so many people out of work that he could not rent his houses would put him out of business. Barring that, he "has it made."

UNIQUE INVESTMENTS

In the last few years it has become popular for individuals with high incomes to buy a wide variety of agricultural land. In the typical case the person has no knowledge whatever of the raising of the particular crop or, in some cases, animals that he is buying. His incentive is actually a "tax dodge." As in all investments, there is money to be made and lost in such a deal. My suggestion is never to approach one of these deals unless you can make money regardless of the tax advantage. There is an old story of a doctor who found a tremendous tax shelter in December. By investing $10,000 he could get an immediate 90 percent write-off. Since he was in the 50 percent tax bracket, this meant he would save $4,500 in cash he would otherwise pay in taxes. His broker warned him not to, but he went ahead anyway. He was right. He did write off 90 percent and save $4,500. But within three months his investment was foreclosed on, and he lost all the money he had invested.

Investment	$10,000
Tax saving	4,500
Actual investment loss	$ 5,500

When you invest in such things as grapes, for example, the government often allows you to write off all the interest on the loan on the property for the year you buy it plus one more year. This is termed prepaid interest. In addition, assuming that the land is bare and you plant grape vines, you are normally allowed to very rapidly depreciate the cost of the planting. This also applies to sheds, barns, fences, and other items essential to growing the crop. Finally, you can usually write off all the fertilizer that you purchase along with pesticides and other plant foods immediately. In the first few years there can be enough write-offs on such a project that an owner who is in a 50 percent tax bracket may have enough tax shelter from his large grape field to write off half of that 50 percent in taxes. If he were making $100,000 a year, this could mean a savings of $25,000 in cash. That does make grapes, avocados, and cabbage appealing, if you are in the right bracket. If you are not, there is no advantage at all unless you particularly want to go into farming.

Furthermore, unless you know a great deal about raising avocados or grapes or whatever or know someone who has this knowledge and will handle the property for you, I would advise you to stear clear of these investments. They may look great on an accountant's figuring pad, but if you end up losing more money than you put in, you are not playing the game to win.

CONVERSIONS

Conversion is taking a piece of property and changing it into something other than what it was when you bought it, presumably with the intention of selling at a profit.

The most successful conversion I ever saw was that of a real estate broker in San Francisco who bought a flat in an area of town zoned R-2. That zoning meant that it was allowable to have two units on each lot. The building he bought was a single residence that was two stories tall (as are most of the residences in San Francisco). What was unusual was that it had a stairway from the street to the second floor as well as a street entrance to the first floor. There was one bathroom upstairs and one downstairs, but only one kitchen, downstairs. The top and bottom floors were connected by another staircase inside.

The broker bought the building for $25,000, closed off the stairway inside, added a kitchen upstairs (which cost him under $3,000), and sold the building within three months for $50,000. (He had doubled its rental potential.)

Conversions, when they work, are a fantastic source of real estate profit. However, let me relate the first conversion my brother, Marc, attempted.

The house was located on Race Street in San Jose, California. Marc was fresh out of college and not willing to listen to, let alone accept, any advice. He felt this was a great deal. Here is the story as I eventually learned it:

The house was on a 50 × 100 lot, had two bedrooms and a bath and a half, and was selling for $5,000 total price. This was not during the depression; this was during the fifties, when any house at all would bring $10,000 to $12,000. The owner wanted only $1,000 down and was willing to take back the entire balance in a first loan. This seemed very generous to Marc, but he was soon to find out why.

He leaped into the deal, borrowing the money from me on a personal-loan basis. He bought the house and immediately went to a bank and asked for a loan of $7,000. After all, the house must be worth at least $10,000, he reasoned, why should they not loan $7,000. They would not loan 10¢.

The bank's appraiser came out and after just a cursory inspection informed Marc that the house had no foundation. The house was old, but he had never bothered to check how old. We later found out it had been there for over 80 years. When it was built, they did not pour concrete as a foundation for a building. They just wet down the mud and laid redwood boards on it. The appraiser told him that no lending institution would lend a dime on a mudsill house. "But it's lasted all this time," he pointed out, to no avail.

He could, of course, simply have rented the place. But he was eager to quickly turn over his property, not to mention return my $1,000 and keep the profits for himself. He decided to convert the house to a duplex.

After examining the house, he decided he could make a front and back conversion. By closing the door to the living room, which was in front, and using it as a bedroom, he could separate the building into two apartments. The back would have a living room, bedroom, bathroom, and kitchen. The front would have a bedroom, a living-dining room, and half a bath, that is, a toilet and sink but no tub or shower. There was room, he reasoned, to put a shower unit in the front bathroom. And on one of the walls of the living room–dining room he thought he would install a sink-oven-stove unit of a type often found in studio apartments. He would make the conversion, get two rents, and sell for a profit, or so he thought.

In order to save money, he decided to do the work himself. From the very first I remember it as a nightmare. The walls of the building were not constructed as walls normally are in buildings today. On the West Coast one can expect a wall to begin with a layer of sheetrock perhaps $\frac{1}{2}$ inch thick, to have 2 × 4 inch studs behind it, and to have an exterior of wood or heavy stucco. The walls on the house on Race Street were two pieces of wood 1 inch thick by 12 inches wide. The first piece of wood ran from the floor upward to support the ceiling.

The second piece of wood was nailed horizontally across the first and anchored at the ends of each wall. There was no space and no studs between them. In addition, layers of burlap and then wallpaper had been pasted as a covering for the wood on the inside. On the outside, the boards had been merely painted with a whitewash.

Undaunted, he plodded on. Going under the house, he rearranged the plumbing in what turned out to be an artistic design so that the front unit had facilities for two more drains (shower and kitchen sink) and outlets for hot and cold water.

It was at this point that I stopped by to see how my money was doing. After sizing up the situation, I asked if he was sure the area was zoned for duplexes. He looked at me inquiringly.

There followed a mad rush by him down to the city planning department and then the information that the block was zoned R-2, for duplexes. He almost wept when he told me, then angrily told me to mind my own business. I did. My brother continued working on the house, and although I dropped in occasionally, thereafter I refrained from making any comments.

During the conversion he could not rent the house, and then his first loan payments became due (not to me, but to the former owners). They were not much, but he was spending all his limited funds on the conversion work. To speed progress, he began working until twelve at night and all weekend. That was his undoing. A neighbor, harassed by the banging and clanking at all hours, called the city and complained. The complaint found its way to the building department, which discovered in due time that there was no permit issued at that moment for work to be done on any house on Race Street.

One Monday, he later related, as he arrived at six o'clock for his evening's work feeling good that the project was almost completed, he found a note tacked to the front door. It requested his presence at the building department at his convenience any time within the next forty-eight hours.

Tuesday morning he was there as soon as they opened the doors and received the following information. The house on Race Street did not meet building codes in the following areas: plumbing, heating, size of windows per room, size of doors per room, structural safety of foundation; and finally, it was a fire hazard because of its wood construction. In short it was condemned. In addition there was the slight problem of his doing work on the building without a permit. Apparently some mention of misdemeanor charges floated through the air, but quickly passed away when he agreed to stop all work and board up the building. He also had to sign an agreement to have the structure torn down or completely rebuilt starting within sixty days. He left in dismay. He subsequently discovered it would cost $12,000 to rebuild, $150 to tear down. The demolition crew arrived two weeks later.

This story does, however, have a happy ending. After the house was wrecked, he put the lot up for sale. It was, after all, an R-2 lot worth more than a simple R-1, or single-family- residence lot. Within a month a builder offered him $5,500 cash. He took the offer.

His expenses on the complete deal in addition to the original purchase price included a shower stall and kitchen unit, neither of which he could return. In addition he had to pay three months interest on the loan to the former owner. The total was $477. After paying back my $1,000, his net profit on the deal was $13. Not much for three months of back-breaking work, worry and despair. But he had gained a world of experience.

Conversions can be fun and profitable. Marc did go on to convert other properties for good returns on his investment. However, now he knew what to look for and how to make conversion work. For the potential investor, here is a set of guidelines to check before investing your money:

1. Are you in compliance with zoning laws?
2. Are you in compliance with building regulations?
3. Exactly what will all construction work cost (including an allowance for inflation)?

4. Do you have adequate reserves to handle the loan, taxes, etc., while the conversion takes place?

5. Do you have a good idea of what rental income you can expect after conversion? Is it enough to allow you a profit on both the rental and eventual sale of the property?

6. Do you yourself know enough about construction to handle a conversion?

If you can answer yes to all these questions, then I would say conversions are an excellent investment for you. If you have even one no, then you had better rethink the deal. Perhaps buying a run-down home and fixing it up might make a better place for you to start, and learn.

NON-REAL ESTATE INVESTMENTS

Stocks

The stock market moves in step with the health of the country. In fact, many consider the stock market the true indicator of how well we are doing economically. It does not take any farsightedness, therefore, to realize that during a modern recession stocks will tend to be depressed. Some have argued, however, that the time to buy is when the price is low. One cannot argue with such assessments. It always is a good policy to buy low and sell high—that is virtually the only way there is to make a profit. The only questions with regard to stocks are which ones do you buy and how long will you have to wait? My feeling is that during uncertain times, investments should be put in the safest possible area commensurate with the potential for high profit. To buy stocks in an uncertain and depressed market is to take large risks. Even when the market rallies, as it is sure to do eventually, the particular stocks you purchase may not gain a lot in value. Finally, if you can double your money in a few years in real estate, it makes no sense at all to put it in stocks, which during those same years may show no gain at all.

Commodities

A brief understanding of the commodity market is necessary in order to understand its perils. When one buys commodities, one is basically buying *futures*. Futures are simply contracts which promise that an investor will either buy or sell a given amount of a commodity for a specific price at some future date. Theoretically futures are bought by two groups of people, those who produce a commodity and those who use it. Commodities can be almost anything—wheat, soybeans, cattle, copper, etc. Futures are sold at various locations including the West Coast Commodity Exchange; the New York Mercantile Exchange; "Comex," New York's Commodity Exchange; and the Chicago Board of Trade. A user or producer of a commodity obtains a future contract to protect himself against the frequent price jumps and declines that occur in the commodity market. The easiest way to see how this works is through an example. Let us take the case of an electronics company that is a user of copper. Assume that copper is selling for $1 a pound and the electronics firm figures it will need 10,000 pounds over the next year. It bases the selling price of the product it makes, minicalculators, on the $1 per pound price of copper. But what if in one year the price of copper should double to $2 a pound? It might be too late for the company to change the prices on its products and it might have to absorb the difference in the form of a loss ($10,000 on 10,000 pounds). The company could, of course, buy the copper now, but that would mean an immediate expenditure of money, plus the problem of storage. The answer is a future buying contract. For a small fee, a broker arranges a contract that basically says the electronics firm will buy 10,000 pounds of copper at a $1 a pound within one year. Now if the cost of copper should increase, the company is protected. It has a guarantee of so much copper at a certain price in the future (the longest term for futures is normally eighteen months). But what if the price of copper should fall? Why would the electronics firm want to buy copper at $1 when a year from now it might be selling on the open market for 95¢?

Why indeed? To protect the contract against such an adverse happening, the broker usually requires a cushion of cash, or "margin," of roughly 9 percent of the contract. If the price should drop to 95¢ now, the broker has the money on hand to guarantee that the electronics firm will honor its contract. If however, the price should start falling even further, the broker would demand more money to maintain the cushion. If the price dropped to 80¢, the electronics firm would have to come up with an additional 20¢. Of course in actual practice it is not necessary to continue following the price down (or up). The firm can "close out" its position at any time before the "contract month" with an offsetting contract—(an agreement, in this case, to sell at $1 a pound or whatever the price is).

Thus far we have been concerned primarily with one side of a futures contract, the buying position of an electronics firm. Now let us consider the other side, that of the company that agrees to sell to the electronics firm the 10,000 pounds of copper at $1 a pound. Very likely this is a copper producer, a mining company. It obtains a selling contract because it is afraid the price of copper might drop within the next year. It bases its labor costs and capital investments on a sales price of $1. If that drops to 50¢ the company could be ruined.

These actions by commodity users and producers are often called "hedging" and their advantages are obvious. Now enters the outside investor. He can neither produce nor use a commodity. He purchases the futures strictly on speculation, hoping that the price will go up, if he is in a buying position, or down, if he is in a selling position. In our example, he buys the contract at $1 per pound for 10,000 pounds of copper to be delivered in twelve months. But he has no intention of taking delivery. In fact, that would be the worst thing that could happen to him for he cannot use copper. Rather, he is gambling that some time before the contract month, the price of copper will go up and he will be able to sell his contract at *over* $1 a pound to a real consumer just entering the market. If he is a "professional" he has spent years studying the market and experience tells him when to buy or sell. Now consider the difference between him and the electronics firm and copper company. If the electronics firm secures a buying position at $1 and the price goes down, it must put up more money to protect its contract (or lose what it has already invested in margin). But even if the price drops to 50¢ and the company loses 50¢ on every pound, it makes up this exact amount *when it purchases the copper to use*. Remember, it was committed to $1 a pound for its pricing policy. If it loses 50¢ a pound on a futures contract but then buys the commodity for 50¢ a pound, it is still at its required $1 per pound cost. The same is true inversely of the mining company. *But it is not true of the outside investor*. If he secures a buying position and the price drops, he cannot make up his loss if the price drops by buying the commodity, for he has no use for it. He simply loses his money. The same holds true for him in a selling position, because if the price rises, he can't take advantage of it. The risk is virtually 100 percent greater for an outside investor than for a consumer or producer of a commodity.

I am reminded of the story of an individual who obtained buying futures in potatoes. His time period was six months, and the price proceeded to drop from the moment he purchased. He was constantly having to come up with more money to meet his margin. He even received a call at three o'clock one Sunday morning from his broker for another $1,500. When his six months were up, the potatoes were selling for roughly one-half the amount he had contracted for. Rather than take a huge loss (remember, he did not stand to lose half the money he invested by selling below his contract price, but all of it), he took delivery of the potatoes, in his apartment, in Manhattan. From then on it seemed that whenever anyone went to dinner in his apartment, potatoes were always a significant portion of the meal.

Gold and Silver

Silver is basically a commodity, for there are many consumers and producers of the metal, and consequently it is subject to much the same perils as any commodity. However, because there is a relatively constant supply of the metal, it is subject to hoarding by speculators. In 1974, for example, purchasing agents reportedly representing Nelson B. Hunt, son of famous Texas oilman H. L. Hunt, apparently made an effort to corner the silver market. Purchasing close to forty million ounces, the price of silver was driven up from around $2 an ounce to over $6 an ounce in a few short months. This, however, drew out huge amounts of hoarded silver, which glutted the market, driving the price down by several dollars an ounce.

Individuals who invest in silver take a double risk. First, there are the perils of a commodity investment, and second, there are the influences of a few large hoarders, which can swing the market in either direction in a very short time. There is no question that there is money to be made by investing in silver, but money can be lost here as well.

Silver and gold have two other problems attached to them. The first is that there is no real government-protected futures market for them as of this writing. This means that the full amount for the silver purchased must be paid in cash at the time it is bought and delivery must be taken, bringing in necessary problems of security and storage.

Gold has all the problems inherent in silver, plus another as well. It is basically not a commodity. There are very few users of gold and, today, very few producers. The supply of the metal is relatively constant, and its price is determined almost entirely by hoarders who keep it off the market. If the United States, for example, were to suddenly dump its holdings of gold (which amount to 37 percent of the free world's supply, or roughly one-fourth of the world's total supply) on the open market, the price would undoubtedly plummet. (This could make a lot of sense for the United States government, because it would be able to suddenly generate a lot of cash, which conceivably would help reduce inflation.)

Investors in gold and silver are basically speculators. They are usually outside of the market and consequently buy high, hoping the price will go higher. It may and then again it may not. If it does, of course they have a profit. If it does not, however, their money is tied up. It does not bring them any income; in fact it costs them money for storage. Their only option here is to sell for a loss. To my mind the profit potential in real estate is just as high while the risk factor is not even one-tenth as high.

Coins and Paintings

Coins and paintings have shown tremendous price increases over the past decade, with some coin issues and certain types of paintings registering gains as high as 60 percent a year every year. However, this is a specialist's field. Some paintings have declined in value. Some coins have not even kept up with inflation. For the individual who is a numismatist or a lover of paintings these are excellent investments. Even if they do not appreciate in value, they will bring untold pleasure and delight to such an owner. But for the outside investor they are highly speculative. Besides being subject to many of the same perils as precious metals, such as the price being determined by hoarding, there is the problem of disposal.

There is no problem selling a rare coin or painting when the market is going up. There are many speculators who are willing to pay high prices on the hope that the value will go even higher and then they can sell for a profit. But when the market begins to dip, there are very few buyers. Not that the speculators do not want to buy; they are waiting, hoping the market will go even lower so that they can buy and at even cheaper prices. If you do not love coins or paintings, stay away from this market.

Novelties

This must truly be the most speculative market of all, for here all the perils of the established markets such as coins and paintings prevail as well as the further peril of a market whose very existence depends on fads. Of course, certain novelties have an established market; however, of late I have seen individuals buy old pinball machines, barber chairs, parking meters, and such as *investments*. It is one thing to buy one of these to have as a novelty in one's home, but to buy three dozen hoping to sell later at enormous profits is unbelievably speculative. I personally feel you would be better off "investing" your money in Las Vegas than in such a field.

10

Conclusion—Liquidity and Leverage

All people should have some real estate investments whether they hope to make a fortune in the field or not. There is nothing which will protect against inflation, provide security against unemployment, and weather the storms of a bad economy like real estate. Among all investments the risks are least great here, yet the potential for profit is among the highest.

However, any investor must keep in mind that all real estate investments are *long term*. By its very nature, real estate is not a liquid asset as are stocks or cash in the bank. Investors should only risk that capital that they can spare for a long period of time—three years at a minimum. That way they will not be in a position of having to sell at a short-term loss because they need money to live on, when they could sell at a profit if they held a few more years. Real estate at first is best purchased as a sideline, as a part-time occupation while the investor works full time at his or her regular occupation. The people who make the most money in real estate began by investing in it in their extra time.

It has often been said that the key to success in real estate is leverage. It is, and then again it is not. In terms of buying a home, as in the Home Reinvestment Plan outlined in Chapter 2, buying with as little down as possible makes sense. But later on, when you are into income-producing property, high leverage does not make sense. Any leverage that finds you putting less than 20 percent down (cash out of your pocket) on an income-producing piece of real estate has every likelihood of being a poor-risk venture. I would estimate that for every 1 percent above 80 that you leverage in this type of property you increase your risk factor by 5 percent. A 90 percent leveraged deal is 50 percent more risky by its very nature than an 80 percent leveraged deal. At 100 percent leverage you double the risk of foreclosure over 80 percent. Keep that in mind the next time your brother-in-law tells you of the fantastic half-million-dollar building you can buy with only $500 cash down.

A modern recession is like a tidal wave. From a small beginning it can bring catastrophic loss of income, loss of security, and even emotional instability to those who are caught up in the fury of it. But to those who can ride the crest, it can be a time of great opportunity and, economically speaking, profit. Are you in the wave or on top of it?

Glossary of Most Commonly Used Real Estate Terms

Here are definitions of the most frequently used real estate terms that you as a buyer or seller of property should be aware of if for no other reason than to protect yourself. Since an exact definition of each term would probably involve more room than is available in this entire book and since some terms mean slightly different things in different areas, an approximation of the most common definition is given here.

ABSTRACT OF TITLE: A summary of all the papers or documents that affect the title to a piece of property. This is usually obtained from a title search company after a deal goes to escrow. It lists all the outstanding loans and all the persons having an interest in the property. It is best to have an experienced broker or lawyer check over an Abstract of Title if you do not know what to look for. If your sale is going to involve title insurance, the title insurance company will normally be more interested in the Abstract of Title than you, the buyer, for this company is guaranteeing your title when the sale closes.

ACCELERATION CLAUSE: A statement sometimes inserted in a mortgage or a trust deed which accelerates the payments if certain conditions come to pass. This simply means that if a piece of property is sold or leased or the title is otherwise affected, the loan will have to be paid off all at once instead of over the period of years otherwise specified. Most modern mortgages carry acceleration clauses. If you have one on the loan on your house, it usually means that the entire loan has to be paid off when you sell. Sometimes the loan company will agree to transfer the loan to the buyer—usually, however, at a higher rate of interest.

ACRE: An area of land which contains 43,560 square feet, or roughly seven to eight lots of 50 × 100 feet plus streets and rights of way.

AD VALOREM: A Latin term simply meaning "based upon value." Property taxes, for example, are usually based on the value of the property.

AGENT: A person authorized to represent another. A broker is the agent in a real estate transaction. See the Chapter 4 discussion of listings for further information.

AGREEMENT OF SALE: A written document or piece of paper in which both the buyer and seller agree to specific terms of the sale of a piece of property. A deposit receipt is a type of agreement of sale.

ALTA TITLE INSURANCE POLICY: A special broad-coverage type of insurance on the title of a piece of property. Lenders often require this as a condition of getting a loan.

APPRAISAL: Basically just an opinion as to the value of a piece of property. Presumably the appraiser has had a great deal of experience and knows where to find facts to back up his appraisal, but ultimately it is still just an educated opinion. Most lending institutions make loans on the basis of their own appraiser's evaluation.

APPURTENANCE: Anything put on land, such as a house, a barn, or a fence. Real estate is basically just the land. When the land is sold, no specific mention need be made of these things, but rather their sale is also assumed. Sometimes sales agreements are written "such and such property and all appurtenances."

ASSIGN: To endorse a promissory note or a lease or other interest to someone else.

ASSUME A LOAN: To take over the mortgage on a piece of property. The buyer assumes personal liability for the payment of the loan for which the property is the security. Most FHA and GI loans are assumable, and so the buyer merely takes these over from the seller. This does not always release the seller from all liability, however.

ATTACHMENT: The seizure of a piece of property by a court.

BALLOON PAYMENT: One payment on an installment loan that is larger than any of the others. It is usually either the first or the last payment, although any payment can be "ballooned" by agreement. A balloon payment is frequently found on second mortgages written to be paid back at "1 percent of the original amount per month." If the original amount were $1,000, the monthly payment would be $10. If the interest is low and the term long enough, it is conceivable that the entire loan could be paid back this way. But consider, at $10 per month it will take 100 months just to pay back the principal on the loan. Add interest to this and you may have to extend it another 100 months. If the interest were at 12 percent per year, the loan could never be paid off, for 12 percent of $1,000 is $120, the total amount of one year's monthly payments. When the loan term was up and the remaining balance came due, the borrower would have a balloon payment of $1,000. There is nothing basically wrong with a balloon payment. It is a useful device in keeping monthly payments down as long as the borrower is aware of it. Balloon payments got a bad name when numbers of buyers, after years of paying off a second note, suddenly discovered that they owed virtually the whole loan amount in one balloon payment.

BLANKET MORTGAGE: A loan covering more than one piece of property.

CAPITAL GAIN: A tax term that means roughly a profit or gain on capital. If capital (money) is invested in land, it means profit on the increase in value of the land, usually realized at sale time.

CAPITALIZATION: A technique for determining how much a piece of income-producing property is worth to a buyer. If an apartment house yields $5,000 a year after expenses and the buyer wants to have a 10 percent return on his investment, he should pay no more than $50,000 for the property (10 percent of $50,000 is $5,000).

CAVEAT EMPTOR: A Latin phrase which translates, "Let the buyer beware." Good advice for investors as it urges them to be cautious. This is not found on any real estate forms, but is commonly spoken.

CHATTEL: Personal property.

CHATTEL MORTGAGE: A loan made with personal property as security.

CLOUD ON THE TITLE: Something which prevents a seller from conveying clear title to a buyer. It could be an old unpaid debt which was recorded on the property or a tax lien.

COMMUNITY PROPERTY: Usually, any property acquired during a marriage through the efforts of the partnership of husband and wife and belonging to both, not separately to either one. Most states have community-property laws.

COMPOUND INTEREST: The kind of interest you get in a bank. You earn interest on the money you invest (deposit) plus interest on the interest you have already received (provided you do not withdraw it).

CONDEMNATION: The usual means by which a state or a city acquires a piece of property it wants for a school, a highway, or a park. The seller is required to sell to the public at what is usually determined by both parties to be a reasonable price. Condemnation is in effect forced sale.

CONDOMINIUMS: Basically these are a cross between an apartment and a house. They have· the physical appearance of an apartment building— several units clustered together. Each unit, however, is sold by the developer rather than rented. The ownership is in fee simple, the highest ownership, and the owner can obtain mortgages on his unit as well as be responsible for the payment of taxes. He has virtually complete control within his unit (as long as what he does in no way damages any other unit), but he has only limited control outside it. For example, if the building has four units, any one unit owner normally has only one-fourth of a vote in deciding when to paint the outside of the building, whom to hire as a gardener, etc. In addition he is responsible for one-fourth of the maintenance bill as well as one-fourth of any other communal expenses.

CREDIT REPORT: A report issued by a private company describing the credit history of an applicant. Most lending institutions require these before they will loan a cent. For clues on how to improve your credit report see Chapter 5 on borrowing money.

DEED: A legal paper transferring the title of a piece of property from seller to buyer. See also *grant deed; quitclaim deed; warranty deed.*

DEED OF TRUST: An abbreviated form of mortgage used primarily along the West Coast and particularly in California. The borrower issues a deed to his property to a neutral third party, or trustee. When he pays back the loan, the lender instructs the trustee to deed the property back to the borrower. If the borrower defaults, the lender instructs the trustee to issue the deed to the lender. The person making the loan under a deed of trust can acquire possession of the property within little more than 100 days after the borrower has defaulted, and he does not have to go through court to do it.

DEFAULT: Failure to pay back a loan. When you are in default, foreclosure is usually not far away.

DEFICIENCY JUDGMENT: A court judgment that lenders can get against you in certain circumstances if you have your property foreclosed and it does not bring enough money in a sale to pay off the outstanding loans. It means that you, the borrower, must now make up the difference.

DEPRECIATION: Loss in value to a piece of property due to any cause. See also *tax depreciation.*

EASEMENT: Someone else's interest in your property. For example, utility companies often have easements over the backs of residential lots that give them the right to maintain their power and phone lines. Technically they can come in and tear out fences, bushes, or other obstacles to gain access to their lines. In actual fact, this rarely if ever happens.

EMPLOYMENT VERIFICATION: A form letter from a borrower's employer, verifying that he or she is employed and stating the exact amount of salary made, which lenders or loan insurers often require the borrower to get in order to obtain government-insured loans and certain types of conventional loans.

ENCUMBRANCE: Any kind of a debt on a piece of property. Anytime you place a loan on a piece of property you encumber it.

EQUITY: The amount of your interest in a piece of property. For example, if the property is worth $25,000 and you owe $20,000, your equity is $5,000.

ESCROW: A deed, money, or property placed in the care of a third, neutral party along with instructions for its disposition, to be released only when the contractual terms are met.

ESCROW OFFICER: A third, neutral party to a deal with whom papers and funds are deposited along with instructions on what to do with them. For example, a buyer, seller, or broker brings a signed deposit receipt to an escrow officer. He looks it over and then writes out instructions exactly as the terms of the deposit receipt specify and in legal language. Then both buyer and seller sign essentially the same document. (There may be some variation according to the different costs buyer and seller must pay.) These documents instruct the escrow officer in what he must do. In general, all the groundwork in a transaction is *not* done by the escrow officer; either buyer or seller or broker must handle this. Finally, an escrow officer can solve no problems between buyer and seller, nor can he close a deal. He can function only *when both buyer and seller are in perfect accord* Also called *escrow holder*.

ESTATE: The extent of a person's interest in property. The term is frequently used as a synonym for *equity*.

FEE SIMPLY ESTATE: In many states, simply the best and highest estate a person can have in property, that is, ownership.

FIRST LOAN (OR MORTGAGE): The one of two or more loans on a piece of property that has definite priority when the loans are paid off in the event of foreclosure. Normally, the loan *recorded* earliest is entitled to first opportunity at whatever money is realized from a forced sale. If there is any money left after the first is paid, the second gets that. If any is left after the second loan is paid, the third gets that, and so on.

FORECLOSURE: The forced sale of a piece of property to cover an unpaid and forfeited debt. A foreclosure may or may not involve court action, depending on whether the loan was a *mortgage* or a *deed of trust*.

GRANT DEED: A deed used most frequently in the Western states, particularly California. The grant deed implies warranties in that by giving it the seller suggests he has title. However, the buyer normally does not sue the seller if it turns out that he did not in fact have clear title. Instead he buys title insurance which protects him from loss. See also *warranty deed*.

GROSS INCOME: The total income from a piece of property before any of the expenses are deducted.

GUARANTEE OF TITLE: Basically an opinion as to the condition of the title on a piece of property backed up by funds to compensate for losses due to errors. Usually issued by a title insurance company.

INTEREST TABLE: Simply a written table giving the amount of monthly payments on loans of various amounts of interest.

JOINT TENANCY: A legal term usually signifying ownership in property by two or more persons that features "right of survivorship."

KEY LOT: In a tract, a lot that has the rear of another lot at one of its sides instead of having the sides of other lots at both it sides. In new tracts, key lots are often sold for less money.

LEASE: In real estate a legal agreement to rent for a specific number of years under specified conditions.

LESSEE: The one who rents under a lease.

LESSOR: The one who owns the property and leases it.

LIEN: An encumbrance on a piece of property, something that ties up the title. Tax liens are frequently placed on properties if taxes are not promptly paid. When this is done, the lien has to be paid off before the property can be sold and clear title given.

MINOR: A person not of legal age. In most states, a person cannot validly sign a contract until he or she reaches legal age. The age requirements differ widely, the youngest I know of being eighteen and the oldest twenty-one years.

MORTGAGE: The most common form of a loan on a piece of property. In exchange for the receipt of money, the property is put up as security. In the event of foreclosure, the borrower usually has at least a year to pay back the money and redeem his property.

MORTGAGEE: The person who makes the loan on a mortgage.

MORTGAGOR: The borrower.

NEGOTIABLE NOTE: A note that can be transferred. One could describe money in this manner. Notes on property are also often negotiable.

NOTICE OF ABANDONMENT: A notice usually filed by a builder when he cannot finish a building.

NOTICE OF COMPLETION: A notice filed by a builder when he has finished work on a building—not required in all states.

NOTICE OF DEFAULT: A notice that a borrower is in default which some states require that a lender file before the foreclosure proceedings can begin.

NOTICE OF NONRESPONSIBILITY: A notice which an owner may file in some states when work is being done on his property (for example, by a lessee) without his authorization.

NOTICE TO QUIT: A notice which normally must be given to tenants before they can be evicted. The time they have to respond varies from locale to locale but is usually less than one week.

PERCENTAGE LEASE: A lease used in commercial buildings, providing that the amount of rent will fluctuate with the amount of business the tenant does. These are also often referred to as "escalator clauses"—the more money the tenant makes, the more his rent escalates.

PLANNING COMMISSION: A public body usually responsible for zoning ordinances and variances.

POINTS (ALSO KNOWN AS DISCOUNT POINTS): A one-time fee often paid when a loan is first obtained. One percent of a loan is 1 point.

POWER OF ATTORNEY: Written authority one person gives another to act in his stead.

PRINCIPAL: A buyer or seller in a deal, but not a broker.

PROBATE SALE: Sale of a piece of property from the estate of a person who has died. A probate sale is often administered by a court.

PROMISSORY NOTE: A promise to pay a specified amount of money on a definite date in the future written down on a piece of paper.

PRORATION: In escrow, division of the taxes, interest, rent, etc., between the parties as of a certain date, usually the closing date of escrow. Normally the seller pays the costs before the date, when he owned the property, the buyer after, when his possession started.

QUITCLAIM DEED: A deed which gives the buyer whatever title the seller has in the property but does not specify what the interest is. No warranty is implied, and the seller does not say he has clear title. The buyer in this case takes the risk. Quitclaim deeds are normally useful documents in clearing a title. For example, say the owner of a house is hospitalized and then does not pay his bill. The hospital can secure a court judgment for the amount due and record a lien on the owner's house. If, subsequently, the owner pays the debt, he has to have some instrument to remove the lien so that he can give clear title in a sale. He has the hospital sign a quitclaim deed

REAL ESTATE BOARD: An organization of brokers and salespeople who usually belong to the National Association of Real Estate Boards (NAREB), now National Association of Realtors.

REALTOR®: A broker who is also a member of the National Association of Real Estate Boards (NAREB), now National Association of Realtors.

RECONVEYANCE: A piece of paper that transfers the title of a piece of property back to its owner after he has paid off a loan—used most frequently with a deed of trust.

RIGHT OF WAY: An easement which grants someone else the right to pass over your property—usually issued at the back of lots to utility companies.

SETUP: An income and expense sheet on a particular piece of property.

SPOUSE: Either a husband or a wife.

STRAIGHT-LINE DEPRECIATION: See Chapter 8 on tax problems.

"SUBJECT TO": Language is used occasionally in a deposit receipt. A buyer may purchase a piece of property "subject to" certain conditions, meaning that the deal will be made only if those conditions are met. The phrase is also used in relation to a loan. A buyer may purchase a piece of property subject to a mortgage. This means he does not assume personal liability for the loan.

SUBLEASE: The lease given by someone who, after you lease your property to him, in turn leases it to someone else. Most leases today specifically prohibit renters from subletting.

SUBORDINATION CLAUSE: A paragraph usually inserted in a second or greater loan which states that the loan can never become a first loan. (In the event of default and sale of property, the loans are paid off in numbered order. The first loan gets first crack at the money, the second loan gets second crack, and so on.) The subordination clause is most often used in the purchase of bare land on which a builder plans to begin a project. He gives the owner so much down and a loan with a subordination clause. Now he can go out and get a construction loan, which becomes the first loan (even though it was placed on the property at a later date). If the builder did not have a clause, he probably would not be able to borrow construction money.

TAX DEPRECIATION: An investor's recovery of the loss in value to his property through physical deterioration which tax rules often allow. The investor is allowed to subtract a part of that loss each year from the income received from the property or, in certain cases, from other income. See Chapter 8.

TERMITE CLEARANCE: A clearance given after a termite report has revealed no infestation or that the termites have been removed. Many times loan companies will not lend money without this clearance.

TERMITE REPORT: Report usually made by a private extermination company stating the amount of termite infestation, if any.

"TIME IS THE ESSENCE": A legal phrase often found in real estate contracts which generally means that all the parties agree to promptly perform whatever they are required to do within the time limits set down.

USURY: Charging abnormally high interest rates. Most states have usury laws which provide penalties for anyone charging above a certain rate of interest on a loan. The rates vary from state to state, but the most common range is between 8 and 10 percent.

VA LOAN: See Chapter 5 on borrowing.

VENDEE: In some areas the term used to describe the buyer.

VENDOR: In some areas the term used to describe the seller.

WARRANTY DEED: A deed giving the title to the buyer. In addition, the seller "warrants" that he will defend the title against any and all outside claims. If sometime after the sale is made it turns out that someone other than the seller had title to the land, the buyer may sue the seller in a court of law for "breach of warranty" to recover the amount he paid and damages. This is a type of deed used frequently today.

Index